COOKING WITH
CHILLIES
PEPPERS
& SPICES

TO MY DEAREST HUSBAND
ROBERT –
AN INTREPID CHILLI EATER AND
ENTHUSIASTIC TASTER

COOKING WITH
CHILLIES
PEPPERS
& SPICES

PHILLIPPA CHEIFITZ

NH
NEW
HOLLAND

This edition published in 1994 by
New Holland (Publishers) Ltd
London • Cape Town • Sydney

ACKNOWLEDGEMENTS
The author and publishers would like to thank the following
for the loan of props for photography: Abode; Art Interiors; Bric-à-Brac Lane;
Colonial Cotton Company; Croc's Dinnerware; Dakota, Stuttafords Town Square;
Foster's; Louis Jansen van Vuuren; Mings; Oakhurst Farm Stall; Peter Visser Interiors;
Shades of Provence; Stuttafords, Claremont; Summer House, Boardmans

ISBN: 1 85368 303 5

New Holland (Publishers) Ltd
37 Connaught Street
London W2 2AZ

EDITOR: Laura Milton
DESIGNER: Petal Muller
COVER DESIGNER: Darren McLean
ASSISTANT DESIGNER: Lellyn Creamer
ILLUSTRATOR: Richard Pooler
PHOTOGRAPHER: Roger Bell
PHOTOGRAPHER'S ASSISTANT: Craig Fraser
FOOD STYLING: Phillippa Cheifitz
FOOD PREPARATION AND PROPPING: Vo Pollard

Typesetting by Struik DTP
in Berkeley, Bembo & Gill Sans
Reproduction by Hirt & Carter (Pty) Ltd
Printed and bound in Singapore by Kyodo Printing Co Pte Ltd

Contents

N/A

Introduction

Ban the bland from your kitchen. This book will show
you how to titillate your taste buds with foods that sing with
the zest of chilli and spice. These dishes – from mildly provocative
to distinctly sadistic – are fired by cuisines from the East to the West,
from Mexico to Morocco, along the Mediterranean and around the
Caribbean. Such exotic, robust fare will add punch to any menu.

PASTA WITH SQUID AND CHILLI CREAM SAUCE (PAGE 32)

CHILLIES & PEPPERS

Chilli peppers are fast becoming the star ingredient in contemporary cuisine. All over America, fresh and healthy Mexican-style salsas, which contain chilli peppers as ingredients, are becoming more popular than ketchup to perk up a variety of dishes – from grilled hamburgers to oven-roasts. Fresh, hot peppers and dried New Mexico chillies have become everyday items in the American supermarket. In parts of the world where there is a strong Malay and Indian presence, one may be sure that fresh and dried chillies will be available in supermarkets and, of course, from Indian grocers.

Chillies and peppers are both members of the large Solanaceae family of plants of the genus *Capsicum*. There are the common red, green and yellow peppers which are rich in vitamins A and C and used as flavouring or simply as vegetables. As opposed to these larger sweet peppers, the bell or banana pepper, or the mild Hungarian paprika pepper, the chilli pepper belongs to the fiery variety. The word 'chilli' comes from the Spanish 'chile' and the Nahuatl 'chilli' and has been used to describe hot peppers since the seventeenth century.

The chilli pepper, native to tropical America, is probably the world's oldest cultivated plant. Wild chillies were eaten by the ancient Mexicans from as early as 7000 BC, and cultivated there from around 5200 BC. By the time Columbus landed in the Americas in 1492, the chilli was known from Mexico to Brazil, and in Chile, Argentina, the West Indies and the Caribbean. Pepper seeds were carried to Spain in 1493 and from there their popularity spread rapidly throughout Europe.

At the time of Columbus, spices were as treasured as gems, and offered a very lucrative trade. As they were not found in Europe, explorers of the fifteenth and sixteenth centuries were all looking for new sea routes to the East – the home of spices. The irony of Columbus' discovery of the Americas is that he was, in fact, looking for the Spice Islands or East Indies and India, as well as hoping to discover a source of black pepper. In consequence, therefore, although the Mexicans called the hot spice they knew by its Nahuatl name, 'chilli', Columbus insisted on calling it 'pepper', and on calling the native Americans 'Indians'.

It was the Portuguese navigators since Da Gama who took the chilli from the New World to the East. In this way, the chilli became the mark of many Asian cuisines – from Thailand, the Sichuan region of China, Malaysia, Singapore and Indonesia to Korea. The Spanish introduced the chilli to India.

TYPES OF CHILLIES

The types of chillies available vary greatly in different parts of the world. As the chilli pepper ripens, most varieties change from green to red or yellow, becoming more mellow in flavour – but not losing their heat. Usually the smaller the chilli, the hotter it will be, with the seeds and ribs being the hottest part of all. The chilli is used both in its fresh and dried form, depending on the variety. Strictly speaking, it is considered a vegetable or fruit when fresh; a spice when dried.

When substituting various types of chilli, replace fresh with fresh, and dried with dried. Use the type of chilli that is most convenient for you. Above all, it is the heat of the chilli that counts.

Cayenne chillies are most common and are found in widespread regions of the world. They are very hot, may be picked either when they are green and/or later when they ripen to red. They may also be used fresh and/or when they have dried and may be ground into powder form.

CAYENNE CHILLIES

Serrano chillies are smaller and much hotter than cayenne chillies. They are used fresh and green in Mexican salsas and are also used extensively in Thai cooking. In addition, they may be canned or pickled. Fresh green cayenne chillies make a good substitute.

SERRANO CHILLIES

Jalapeño chillies are grown in Texas and Mexico and are the most widely used fresh, hot chillies in the United States. They are dark green, fatter than the slim cayenne chilli, and wonderfully hot and sweet at the same time. Generally, they don't dry well, but they may be preserved by canning, pickling or smoking. In Mexico, a smoked jalapeño chilli is called a 'chipotle'.

JALAPENO CHILLIES

POBLANO CHILLIES

Poblano chillies are dark green and the same size and shape as sweet bell peppers. In Mexico and Texas they are used fresh, but they are also available in canned form. When preserved by smoking and drying, they darken and wrinkle and are called either **mulato** or **ancho** chillies. The **ancho chilli** is the most common dried chilli in Mexico. Fresh poblano chillies are enjoyed stuffed and baked in Mexican cooking. If you are unable to obtain fresh poblanos, use fresh sweet peppers instead, adding fresh hot chillies to the stuffing to give your dish the bite of the real thing.

PASILLA CHILLIES

Pasilla chillies are dried Mexican chillies that are very dark in colour, even when they are fresh. They are similar to the ancho chilli, but are longer and thinner.

Bird or **birdseye chillies** are small, round and fiery. They are used when they are fresh and/or when ripe and red in Thailand, Indonesia and Malaysia. In South Africa, they grow well on the Cape Flats near Cape Town. In Mexico, they are used fresh or dried, and are called either 'chiliquin' or 'chitecpin'. In the south-western parts of the United States they are also commonly known as **pequin chillies**.

BIRD OR BIRDSEYE CHILLIES

Scotch bonnet chillies are extremely hot, lantern-shaped, and measure about 4 cm (1³⁄₅ in) in diameter. They are used fresh, when yellow, orange or red. They are found in the Caribbean and their distinctive aroma is the mark of West Indian cooking. They are chopped into relishes, or used whole in cooking to soften the bite of a dish.

HANDLING & USING CHILLIES

Be careful when handling chillies. Never touch your face or eyes, and always wash your hands well afterwards. Under cold running water, pull out the stem and split the chilli, removing the inner membranes and seeds. These are the hottest parts of the chilli, and may be included if you like a fiery taste. Otherwise you may want to discard them.

Fresh chillies may be used whilst they are still green, or you may prefer to wait until they are ripe and red. Dried chillies may be softened in boiling water for about 20 minutes or longer before using. Use chillies to make pastes for use in cooking (see right and next page) or to put on the table to hot up a variety of dishes.

STORING CHILLIES

Wash and dry the chillies. Store in small jars and cover with olive or sunflower oil, or with dry sherry. Keep jars in the refrigerator. The oil and sherry may be used on their own for flavouring foods.

MAKING CHILLI FLOWERS

Chillies, cut into 'flower' shapes, make an attractive garnish for hot and spicy foods. Using a sharp knife, slit the fresh chillies lengthwise at equal intervals, leaving about 2.5 cm (1 in) intact at the stem end. Carefully scrape out the membranes and wash out the seeds under cold running water. Soak the chillies in a bowl of iced water for at least an hour until curled.

MAKING CHILLI PASTES

It is always convenient to have a variety of chilli pastes on hand. Pounded chillies are mixed with garlic and spices to flavour cooked dishes or put on the table as relishes to add fire according to personal taste. Chilli pastes keep well, either covered with oil and refrigerated, or when they are frozen.

HARISSA PASTE

This is the popular chilli paste of Morocco. Here is one version, but recipes differ from region to region, and from one cook to another.

125 g (4 oz) whole, dried
red chillies
1 clove garlic
30 ml (2 tbsp) cumin seeds
5 ml (1 tsp) ground coriander
salt
olive oil

Cover the chillies with boiling water and leave to soften for an hour. Drain and pound in a food processor together with the garlic, cumin seeds, coriander and a little salt to make a smooth paste. Thin down with a few spoonfuls of olive oil if necessary. The paste lasts in the refrigerator for weeks if it is kept covered with a film of oil.

FRESH CHILLI PASTE

45 g (1½ oz) chopped, fresh chillies
75 ml (2½ fl oz) olive oil
3 cloves garlic, chopped
15 ml (1 tbsp) ground cumin
15 ml (1 tbsp) ground coriander
a pinch of salt

Simply mix the ingredients and pound to a smooth paste in a small food processor. Transfer the paste to a suitable container, cover with a film of oil and store it in the refrigerator. It will keep for weeks.

DRIED CHILLI PASTE

a dozen dried, red chillies
45 ml (3 tbsp) olive oil
3 cloves garlic, chopped
a good pinch of salt

Split a dozen dried, red chillies. Cover with boiling water and leave them to stand for about an hour until soft. Drain, then pound to a smooth paste in a food processor, adding the oil, garlic and a good pinch of salt. Transfer the paste to a suitable container, cover with a film of oil and store in the refrigerator. It will keep for weeks.

MALAYSIAN DRIED CHILLI PASTE

100 g (3½ oz) dried, red chillies
water

First remove the stems from the dried red chillies. Place the chillies in a saucepan, three quarters filled with cold water. Bring to the boil and simmer for about 5 minutes. Remove from the heat, cover and allow to steep for about 10 minutes. Drain the chillies, wash well and drain again. Blend or process the chillies with 250 ml (8 fl oz) water to form a paste. Refrigerate or freeze and use the paste as needed.

CHILLI POWDER

Ready-made chilli powders are convenient, but they can vary a great deal in content. American and Mexican chilli powders usually contain a mix of different kinds of chillies with cumin or other spices and differ from Indian and African chilli powders. If possible, make a note of what the chilli powder contains and choose the one that is most suited to the dish you are preparing. Fastidious cooks grind their own pure chilli powder to make sure that they know precisely what they are using.

SPICES

It is hard to believe that so much effort was involved in obtaining the spices we use so frequently today: cinnamon and nutmeg, ginger and allspice, cumin and coriander, cardamom and cloves, saffron and turmeric. It was the competence of the navigators that enabled small nations to develop into such vast and wealthy empires.

Spices have long been prized for their qualities as preservatives as well as for their wonderful fragrance and flavours. They were used for thousands of years throughout Asia, the Orient and the Mediterranean region. They are even referred to in the Bible. For centuries the Arabs were the foremost traders, guarding their trade secrets zealously from rival traders and customers alike.

In the first century AD, spices were taken across Asia from China to Europe along ancient caravan trails such as the Silk Road. At the same time the Romans were sailing to India from Egypt – a long and dangerous journey taking years – but they managed to bring back a valuable cargo of spices. With the fall of Rome, Constantinople became the capital of the powerful Eastern Roman Empire and the bustling centre of spice trading between the East and the West.

By the fourteenth century Venice had established the monopoly, supplying the Crusaders. But all this changed in 1498 when Vasco da Gama, the Portuguese explorer, reached India. By the beginning of the sixteenth century the Portuguese had established a network of more than fifty trading posts from Africa to Japan.

During the early seventeenth century it was the turn of the Dutch to become important distributors of spices in Europe. By 1602 they had established themselves in the East as the Dutch East India Company, creating the beginnings of a mighty empire which took over the monopoly of the spice trade. This lasted until the late eighteenth century when the market began becoming more competitive and spices became more affordable.

A QUICK ABC OF SPICES

Spices consist of the fruits, seeds, bark or roots of a great variety of plants. They are used fresh or dried. For the best flavour, buy whole spices and grind as needed in a coffee grinder used only for this purpose. Ready-ground spices are never as aromatic and don't keep as well – usually not for more than three months – stored in an airtight container in a cool place. Whole spices keep for up to a year. To bring out the flavour of the spices, they should be fried in hot oil for 2–3 minutes, or dry-roasted in a heavy pan, being constantly stirred, for about 5 minutes before grinding.

Allspice is made from the whole, unripe berries of the tropical allspice or pimento tree which was first discovered by Columbus in 1494. The berries are dried and available both whole and ground. Allspice gets its name from the flavour which seems like a mix of cinnamon, cloves and nutmeg.

Aniseed consists of the seeds of the anise plant of the parsley family, which is native to the Mediterranean area. It has a strong liquorice flavour and has been popular for many centuries as an aid to digestion.

Caraway seeds are the crescent-shaped, seed-like fruits of a plant similar to parsley. They have a distinctive pleasant flavour with sweet undertones.

Cardamom is native to India, but was grown as early as 721 BC in the garden of the King of Babylon. The small, three-sided, creamy white or green cardamom pod itself has no flavour, but contains tiny, aromatic, dark brown seeds. The seeds have a sweet aroma and pungent flavour most suitable for curries.

Cassia consists of the reddish-brown bark of the cassia tree. It is also available in ground form. It is sometimes referred to as Chinese cinnamon, as it comes from China and is very similar to cinnamon.

Cinnamon comes from Sri Lanka and Malabar and consists of pieces of curled bark from the cinnamon tree, which belongs to the laurel family. It is available whole (called 'sticks') or in ground form. It has a versatile sweet, woody flavour with a distinctive fragrance.

Cloves consist of the dried, unopened flower buds of a tropical tree of the myrtle family. Whole cloves resemble nails and their name comes from the French word 'clou' meaning nail. Cloves are reddish-brown in colour and may be ground.

Coriander is native to southern Europe and the Mediterranean region and its use is mentioned in the Bible. Both the fresh green leaves (called 'cilantro') and seeds are used, although the flavours are quite different. The plant belongs to the parsley family and has a slight lemon flavour. Coriander seeds, which are also available in ground form, cannot be used in place of fresh coriander leaves.

Cumin consists of the small, dried, yellowish-brown seed-like fruit of a plant of the parsley family which is found in India and North Africa. It is available whole and ground and is similar to the caraway seed.

Curry leaves are the pungent leaves of the curry bush, a relative of the lemon tree. The leaves impart a distinctive curry odour when bruised.

Fenugreek comes from the pod of a scented legume. The ground seeds are used as an ingredient for curry powder. Their strong, aromatic smell is similar to celery.

Ginger consists of the rhizome of a tropical plant. Marco Polo recorded finding ginger in China. It is used fresh in spiced and curried dishes. Ginger may also be dried and ground or left in pieces. It may even be crystallized or preserved in syrup, in which case it is used as a confection or condiment, not as a spice. Ginger has a warm aroma with a hot flavour.

Nutmeg and mace are different parts of the same spice. Mace is the outer brownish-orange coating of the nutmeg, the fruit of a tropical tree. Both nutmeg and mace have a sweet, aromatic taste. Traditionally mace, which has a more delicate taste, is used in savoury dishes while nutmeg is used in sweet dishes.

Paprika is native to Central America, but is grown commercially in places like California. It is made from the dried, stemless pod of a sweet red pepper which belongs to the same family as the hot cayenne pepper. Recent research has shown that the plant offers a richer source of vitamin C than citrus fruits. Paprika is a mild, sweet spice which is available in ground form as an orange-red powder.

Pepper is said to be the world's most popular spice. It is made from the dried berries of a vine which is native to the East Indies. Black pepper is made from berries picked just before they are ripe, when they turn black and shrivel. The hotter white pepper is made from berries which are allowed to ripen before harvesting. The outer shell is removed and the greyish-white kernel is dried. To obtain the best flavour, store the whole, dried berries and grind when needed.

Saffron is the most expensive spice of all and is native to the Mediterranean area. It is made from the dried stigmas of the purple, flowering saffron crocus and it is estimated that approximately 75,000 blossoms are needed to make one pound of this spice. Saffron powder is bright yellow and has a distinct, musty flavour. The less expensive turmeric (see below) is often used as a substitute.

Turmeric is native to China and is used extensively in East Indian cookery. It has a golden yellow colour and is used to add colour to foods. It is made from the dried, ground root or rhizome of a plant of the ginger family. Turmeric is aromatic with a mild flavour, but it should be used judiciously as it has a rather bitter taste.

Star anise consists of the dried, star-shaped pods of a small evergreen tree of the magnolia family. It has a sweet, aromatic liquorice taste and is one of the few spices commonly used in Chinese cookery.

NOTES ON EXOTIC INGREDIENTS

Asian shrimp paste (sometimes called 'belakan') is usually available from specialist grocers in jars, cans or packages. This pungent, salty paste lasts very well and should only be used in small amounts. If it is unobtainable, you can make do with pounded, salted anchovies.

Coconut milk is best made from fresh coconut, although it is easier to use dried coconut. Quickest of all is canned coconut milk, or sachets of coconut cream that are reconstituted with boiling water.

If you are using a fresh coconut, prod each of the three eyes with a skewer to find the weakest one. Drain the liquid and discard. This is not milk, it's the water. Bake the coconut at 200 °C (400 °F; gas 6) for 15 minutes, then break it open using a hammer. Remove the flesh from the shell, using the point of a strong knife. Use a vegetable peeler to remove the brown skin. Cut the flesh into small pieces and grate or process in small batches.

To make thick coconut milk, pour 250 ml (8 fl oz) of boiling water over 200 g (7 oz) of freshly grated coconut (or desiccated coconut) and blend in a food processor or blender. Allow to stand for 15 minutes. Turn into a strainer over a bowl, squeezing by hand to extract as much milk as possible. Thin coconut milk is made by repeating the process using the same grated coconut.

Screwpine leaves are the narrow, shiny, sword-like leaves of the screwpine tree, which is native to southern Asia. Screwpine is used as a flavouring in Malay, Thai and Indonesian cooking, particularly in rice dishes. It is sometimes possible to obtain fresh leaves from specialist Oriental shops. Leaves should be kept in the refrigerator – they will

CLOCKWISE: *GARLIC, SPRING ONION, LEMON GRASS, CORIANDER LEAVES, GREEN PEPPER, CURRY LEAVES, PINK PEPPERCORNS, CORIANDER SEEDS, STAR ANISE, FRESH CHILLIES, CINNAMON BARK*

last for a week or two. Dried screwpine leaves, which are less fragrant than fresh leaves, are sold cut into short, curled lengths.

Tamarind juice is made from tamarind, which is available at speciality Indian grocers. To make the juice, mix a nut-sized lump of tamarind with 75 ml (2½ fl oz) of hot water. Allow to stand for about 20 minutes until softened, stirring now and again. Strain through a fine sieve, pushing through the pulp.

Thai fish sauce, which is also called 'Naam Pla', is an essential ingredient in Thai cooking. It is used for seasoning in much the same way as soy sauce in China and Japan. This sauce, made from fermented fish, is usually obtainable from speciality oriental shops. If you are unable to obtain it, you can make do with 15 ml (1 tbsp) of soy sauce blended with a salty anchovy fillet.

Lemon grass is best when it is fresh. A good nursery should be able to supply you with a plant. The fleshy, fibrous lemon grass stalk is slightly larger than a spring onion. Fresh stalks are also sold in bundles of approximately 18–20 cm (7–8 in) long. The stalk ends are trimmed, and the stalks themselves are finely sliced. Lemon grass will keep for about 2–3 weeks in the refrigerator and may be chopped and frozen in a plastic bag. It is also available dried. If unobtainable, use finely chopped lemon peel instead.

CONVERSION FROM METRIC UNITS

Some people prefer using cups and spoons rather than metric units when measuring liquids. The information below may aid conversion.

125 ml = ½ cup   250 ml = 1 cup

Starters & Snacks

Spicy nibbles are nice. Choose one or two from this chapter to start a meal or introduce a few along with your old favourites next time friends come over for drinks. They are especially good with chilled Mexican beer or with a tequila-based cocktail, such as the popular Margarita.

COCKTAILS FOR A CROWD: BABY CORN WITH CHILLI DIP (PAGE 15), TACO CHIPS WITH AVOCADO RELISH AND TOMATO AND BASIL SALSA (PAGE 14), PRAWNS WITH CHILLI SEAFOOD SAUCE (PAGE 14) AND MUSSELS WITH CURRY MAYONNAISE (PAGE 14)

FRESH CORN TERRINE WITH TOMATO CHILLI SAUCE

This unusual terrine makes an elegant starter. The pale yellow of the corn contrasts attractively with the red of the sauce and the green of the coriander leaf garnish. It also makes a good main course for vegetarians, served with a mixed green salad and strips of crisp baby vegetables.

CORN TERRINE
450 g (1 lb) fresh corn kernels
250 ml (8 fl oz) thin (single) cream
5 extra large eggs
a pinch of sugar
salt and freshly ground black pepper

TOMATO CHILLI SAUCE
30 g (1 oz) butter
1 medium onion, finely chopped
1 stick celery, finely chopped
1 clove garlic, crushed
2 cans (about 400 g/14 oz each)
tomatoes, crushed
5 ml (1 tsp) sugar
5 ml (1 tsp) chilli paste (see page 8)
salt and freshly ground black pepper

GARNISH
fresh coriander leaves

To make the corn terrine, blanch the corn kernels in a saucepan of boiling water and drain well. Blend in a food processor with the cream, eggs, sugar and seasoning. Now pour into a 1.5-litre (2¾-pint) loaf tin lightly brushed with oil. Cover with a piece of buttered greaseproof paper and place in a larger baking tin. Pour enough boiling water into the larger tin to reach halfway up the sides. Bake at 150 °C (300 °F; gas 2) for about 1½ hours or until a tester comes out clean. Serve warm or allow to cool to room temperature.

To make the tomato chilli sauce, melt the butter and cook the onion and celery gently for approximately 5–10 minutes. Stir in the garlic, then the crushed tomatoes, sugar and chilli paste. Add a small amount of seasoning and simmer, uncovered, for 15–20 minutes or until slightly reduced. Check the seasoning and adjust if needed,

To serve, unmould the terrine and slice into 6–8 portions. Pour the hot sauce over and garnish with coriander leaves.
SERVES 6–8

SPANISH SHRIMPS IN SPICY TOMATO SAUCE

Make sure that there is a good crusty loaf or hot garlic bread to mop up the sauce. A robust way to start, it also makes a main course, served in generous quantities.

30 ml (2 tbsp) olive oil
1 medium onion, finely chopped
1 clove garlic, crushed
5 ml (1 tsp) chilli powder or paste
(see pages 8–9)
1 can (about 400 g/14 oz) tomatoes
60 ml (4 tbsp) dry white wine
1 bay leaf
15 ml (1 tbsp) finely chopped parsley
sugar to taste
300 g (11 oz) peeled shrimps
(cooked or frozen)

If the shrimps are frozen, see that they are properly defrosted, well drained and dried. Heat the oil in a wide saucepan. Add the onion and cook gently until softened. Stir in the garlic and chilli. Crush the canned tomatoes in a blender or use a potato masher, and add to the saucepan, together with the juice,

the wine, bay leaf and parsley. Cook, uncovered, for approximately 20 minutes or until reduced and thickened. Check seasoning and, if necessary, add a little sugar. Add the shrimps and cook quickly for 1–2 minutes until just cooked and piping hot. Serve immediately.
SERVES 3–4 AS AN APPETIZER

THAI-STYLE FISH CAKES

These are a popular snack in Thailand, a land of endless snacking, perfectly possible in a place where street food is available on every corner.

2 fresh red chillies, chopped
2 cloves garlic, crushed
1 stalk lemon grass, crushed and
chopped (see page 11), or the finely
grated rind of a lemon or lime
15 ml (1 tbsp) Thai fish sauce
(see note)
500 g (18 oz) fish fillets, finely
chopped
125 ml (4 fl oz) coconut milk
(see page 11)
1 extra large egg
oil for frying

NOTE: This is usually available ready-made from speciality oriental shops. If unobtainable, see Notes on Exotic Ingredients (page 11).

In a food processor, pound the chillies, garlic, lemon grass or lemon or lime rind and the fish sauce until smooth. Add the fish and pound until smooth. Blend in the coconut milk and egg. Refrigerate overnight or for a few hours until stiff enough to handle. Shape into small cakes and shallow-fry in hot oil until crisp and brown on both sides. Drain well. The fish cakes are eaten on their own as a snack.
SERVES 4

TACO CHIPS WITH AVOCADO RELISH & TOMATO & BASIL SALSA

Serve a bowl of taco chips with a choice of two Californian dips and chilled Mexican beer.

a bowl of taco chips

AVOCADO RELISH
2 large, ripe avocados, chopped
30 ml (2 tbsp) lemon juice
30 ml (2 tbsp) chopped red onion
1 fresh chilli, chopped
1 clove garlic, crushed
salt and freshly ground black pepper

TOMATO AND BASIL SALSA
250 g (9 oz) firm, red tomatoes,
seeds removed, chopped
1 fresh, red chilli, chopped
30 ml (2 tbsp) chopped red onion
30 ml (2 tbsp) balsamic vinegar
15 ml (1 tbsp) olive oil
1 clove garlic, crushed
30 g (1 oz) basil leaves, shredded
salt and freshly ground black pepper

Combine the necessary ingredients to make the relish and the salsa. Serve a bowl of taco chips with a choice of these two dips.
SERVES 6

PRAWNS WITH CHILLI SEAFOOD SAUCE

This is a perfect appetizer for prawn lovers – they'll love the traditional sauce perked up with chilli.

250 g (9 oz) frozen prawn tails

SAUCE
60 ml (4 tbsp) thick soured cream
60 ml (4 tbsp) thick mayonnaise
15 ml (1 tbsp) tomato sauce
5 ml (1 tsp) chilli paste (see page 8)
a dash of Tabasco sauce

Drop the frozen prawn tails into boiling water for barely a minute until pink and curled. Allow to cool, then peel off the shells leaving the tails intact. To make the sauce, combine all the ingredients and mix well. Pass round the prawn tails with the sauce as a dip.
SERVES 4–6 AS COCKTAILS

SPICY COCKTAIL CHICKEN WINGS

These spicy titbits make great appetizers. For a more substantial snack, bake the wings whole and serve with a crunchy coleslaw.

16 chicken wings

MARINADE
30 ml (2 tbsp) sunflower oil
15 ml (1 tbsp) honey
5 ml (1 tsp) chilli paste (see page 8)
15 ml (1 tbsp) soy sauce
15 ml (1 tbsp) apple cider vinegar
1 clove garlic, crushed
a slice (1.5 cm/½ in) of fresh root
ginger, peeled and crushed

Remove wing tips and cut the wings in half at the joint. Arrange in a single layer on an oiled baking tray. Combine the marinade ingredients and mix well. Pour over the chicken and marinate for a few hours or overnight, turning over once or twice. Bake at 200 °C (400 °F; gas 6) for 40 minutes or until browned and tender. If you like, thread onto thin bamboo skewers for serving. Serve warm or at room temperature.
SERVES 16 AS A COCKTAIL SNACK

MUSSELS ON THE HALF-SHELL WITH CURRY MAYONNAISE

Plump mussels marry well with a spicy mayonnaise, and look wonderfully decorative when served on the half-shell.

500 g (18 oz) steamed mussels
on the half-shell

CURRY MAYONNAISE
125 ml (4 fl oz) thick mayonnaise
5 ml (1 tsp) curry powder
(see page 71)
5 ml (1 tsp) chutney
a grinding of black pepper

GARNISH
fresh coriander leaves

Remove the mussels from the shell and set aside. Mix the ingredients for the curry mayonnaise well. Place a dab of the mayonnaise mixture into each half-shell and top with a mussel. Tuck in a coriander leaf.
SERVES 6 AS COCKTAILS

BARBECUE SPARERIBS WITH CHINESE CHILLI SAUCE

This is a very good method of preparing the spareribs. To make a meal of them, allow two people to share a rack of ribs. Add baked potatoes and a salad of baby spinach leaves.

1 rack spareribs

MARINADE
2 cloves garlic, crushed
15 ml (1 tbsp) clear honey
15 ml (1 tbsp) water
15 ml (1 tbsp) vinegar
45 ml (3 tbsp) soy sauce
2.5 ml (½ tsp) chilli paste
(see pages 8–9)

SPICY CEVICHE (PAGE 16) AND FRESH CORN TERRINE WITH TOMATO AND CHILLI SAUCE (PAGE 13)

Combine the ingredients for the marinade and mix together well. Place the spareribs with the marinade in a plastic bag. Close and place the bag in a suitably long, shallow container. Leave in the refrigerator for a day or more, turning the bag now and again.

Remove the spareribs from the bag and place them on a rack over a roasting tin filled with water. Roast at 190 °C (375 °F; gas 5) for about 45 minutes; then increase the temperature to 230 °C (450 °F; gas 8) and roast for a further 15 minutes or until crisp and browned. Chop into separate ribs and serve hot, with ready-made Chinese chilli sauce poured over.

SERVES 4 AS A STARTER

BABY CORN WITH CHILLI DIP

The sweetness of corn contrasts deliciously with the bite of a chilli dip.

250 g (9 oz) steamed baby corn

CHILLI DIP
60 ml (4 tbsp) ready-made chilli sauce
60 ml (4 tbsp) thick mayonnaise
15 ml (1 tbsp) chopped fresh coriander

Combine the ingredients for the chilli dip and mix them thoroughly. Then simply pass round the hot corn and the accompanying dip.

SERVES 4–6 AS A COCKTAIL SNACK

GRILLED NACHOS

This is an irresistible snack – crunchy, corn-based chips topped with melted cheese and tomato.

250 g (9 oz) large taco chips or nachos
1 can (about 400 g/14 oz) Mexican-style tomatoes with chilli (see note on page 41)
125 g (4 oz) grated Cheddar cheese

Arrange taco chips or nachos in a single layer on a baking tray or microwave platter. Spoon some tomato onto each chip. Cover with grated cheese. Grill or microwave just until the cheese melts.

SERVES 4–6

SPICY CEVICHE

Ceviche comes from South America, and appears in many variations. Absolutely fresh fish is marinated in lime or lemon juice, which actually 'cooks' the fish, turning the flesh opaque.

500 g (18 oz) filleted fresh white fish
(or fresh tuna)
250 ml (8 fl oz) fresh lime
or lemon juice
2 firm, red tomatoes, finely chopped
1 bunch spring onions, thinly sliced
2 fresh chillies, seeds removed,
finely chopped
1.25 ml (¼ tsp) chilli powder
(see page 9)
60 ml (4 tbsp) olive oil
30 ml (2 tbsp) white wine vinegar
2.5 ml (½ tsp) dried oregano
15 ml (1 tbsp) chopped fresh
coriander leaves
salt and freshly ground black pepper

GARNISH
1 large, firm avocado, thinly sliced
fresh coriander leaves

Use fish that is absolutely fresh and sliced thinly across the grain. Place the fish in a bowl (not a metal one) and pour the lemon or lime juice over. Cover and refrigerate for a few hours. Now add the remaining ingredients and mix well. Check seasoning and add salt and pepper if necessary. Cover and chill until serving. Garnish with avocado slices and fresh coriander leaves.
SERVES 4–6

PITTA BREADS WITH SPICY CHICKEN LIVERS

Pitta breads are excellent with warm spicy fillings. This recipe makes a hearty snack or light meal. For cocktails, use miniature pittas.

2 pitta breads
shredded lettuce
fresh coriander leaves

SPICY CHICKEN LIVERS
500 g (18 oz) chicken livers
45 ml (3 tbsp) oil
2 cloves garlic, crushed
1 fresh, red chilli, split
1 medium onion, finely chopped
5 ml (1 tsp) paprika
5 ml (1 tsp) cumin
salt and freshly ground black pepper

To make the spicy livers, trim and quarter the livers and pat dry using paper towels. In a wide pan, heat the oil gently with the garlic and chilli. Add the onion and cook gently for about 10 minutes until softened and golden. Stir in the paprika and cumin. Increase the heat and add the livers. Sauté quickly until nicely browned outside but still pinkish inside. Season to taste. Discard the chilli at this point.

To assemble, warm the pitta breads under a grill or in a microwave. Then, using a sharp knife, make a slit in each – wide enough to push in the filling. First push in shredded lettuce, then the piping hot spicy chicken livers and some coriander leaves to finish. Serve immediately.
SERVES 2 AS A SUBSTANTIAL SNACK

BAKED SPICY CORN CAKE

This is rich and delicious, but worth every calorie. It makes a marvellous main course served with a green salad, lightly tossed in oil and lemon juice.

15 ml (1 tbsp) sunflower oil
500 g (18 oz) spicy sausage, sliced
1 medium onion, finely chopped
3 extra large eggs
250 ml (8 fl oz) soured cream
250 ml (8 fl oz) milk
125 g (4 oz) coarse, yellow corn meal
60 g (2 oz) flour
10 ml (2 tsp) baking powder
3 fresh or bottled chillies,
finely chopped
250 g (9 oz) mild Cheddar
cheese, grated
225 g (8 oz) fresh corn kernels
salt and freshly ground black pepper
butter for baking

Heat the oil in a large, heavy pan and lightly brown the sausage. Then, using a slotted spoon, remove to an oiled 30-cm (12-in) round baking dish. Add the onion to the pan, with a small amount of oil if necessary, and cook gently until softened. Spoon over the sausage. Beat the eggs, soured cream and milk together. Mix the corn meal, flour, baking powder and 2.5 ml (½ tsp) salt. Now beat in the egg mixture. Stir in the chillies, cheese and corn. Add a grinding of pepper. Pour this mixture over the sausage and onion. Dot with butter and bake at 180 °C (350 °F; gas 4) for about 45 minutes or until golden and set. Allow to stand for 5–10 minutes before cutting. For cocktails, cut into small squares.
SERVES 8 AS A SNACK OR STARTER

The taco – probably Mexico's most popular culinary export – is a freshly made warm tortilla rolled around a filling and eaten by hand. A tray of tacos, a choice of fillings (see pages 18–20) and a variety of toppings (see page 21) make a fun fiesta for a crowd of friends, or an easy supper for the family.

FOR A TEX-MEX PARTY: *TOMATO AND CORN SALSA* (*PAGE 54*), *CHILLI AND BEANS FOR A CROWD* (*PAGE 54*) *AND GRILLED NACHOS*

TACO FILLINGS

The name taco comes from the Spanish word for 'snack' or 'bite to eat'. In Mexico the soft taco is favoured. Crisp, deep-fried tacos are more popular in so-called Tex-Mex cooking, which consists of Texan adaptations of Mexican dishes.

The hot taco filling is topped with crisp shredded lettuce, salsa, guacamole, grated cheese and thick, soured cream. Monterey Jack cheese is used extensively in the United States, but adequate local substitutes are available. You can also make up a mix of grated Cheddar and mozzarella. Pass round extra hot chilli sauce.

SHREDDED BEEF FILLING

This is the way Mexicans love to prepare the meat for taco fillings. Beef shin is wonderfully gelatinous and stands up to long, slow cooking better than topside, which tends to dry out. The tender meat is not chopped, but pulled apart into shreds by hand or by using forks.

STEP 1
1 kg (2¼ lb) boneless beef shin
750 ml (1¼ pints) water or stock
4 cloves garlic
2 fresh chillies, chopped
salt and freshly ground black pepper

STEP 2
30 ml (2 tbsp) sunflower oil
2 medium onions, sliced
2 cloves garlic, crushed
1 chilli, chopped

STEP 1 Place the beef in a heavy casserole dish. Pour over the water or stock. Then add the garlic, two chopped chillies, and a little salt and pepper. Cover tightly and bake at 160 °C (325 °F; gas 3) for 2–3 hours or until fork-tender. Remove from the oven and allow to cool in the liquid. Once cool enough to handle, shred by hand or by using a fork. Return meat to the strained broth.

STEP 2 Heat the oil in a frying pan. Add the onion and cook for about 5 minutes or until softened and lightly browned. Stir in the garlic and chopped chilli and cook for 1–2 minutes. Add to the meat and broth. Over a high heat, cook for a further 5 minutes or until slightly reduced. Season to taste.
SERVES 6

SPICY CHILLI MINCE

This is an excellent basic recipe, full of flavour with its mix of spices and herbs.

60 ml (4 tbsp) sunflower oil
2 medium onions, chopped
3 cloves garlic, crushed
1 kg (2¼ lb) lean, minced beef
1 red pepper, seeds removed, chopped
1 green pepper, seeds removed, chopped
2 fresh chillies, chopped
15 ml (1 tbsp) ground coriander
15 ml (1 tbsp) ground cumin
5 ml (1 tsp) ground cinnamon
2.5 ml (½ tsp) ground allspice
30 ml (2 tbsp) chilli powder
(see page 9)
5 ml (1 tsp) fresh oregano
60 ml (4 tbsp) chopped parsley
2 cans (about 400 g/14 oz each) tomatoes
45 ml (3 tbsp) tomato paste
salt and freshly ground black pepper
1–2 cans (about 400 g/14 oz each) pinto or red kidney beans (optional)

GARNISH
fresh coriander leaves

Heat the oil in a heavy casserole dish. Add the onions and cook very gently until softened. Stir in the garlic. Increase the heat and add the mince. Keep stirring until the meat changes colour. Stir in the chopped peppers and chillies, the herbs and spices and some seasoning. Mix in the crushed tomatoes plus the juice from the can and the tomato paste. Cover, reduce the heat and cook very gently, stirring now and again, for an hour or longer until the meat is very tender. Season to taste. If using, add the beans and allow to heat through. Sprinkle with fresh coriander leaves.
SERVES 10–12

SHREDDED PORK FILLING

Pork is used extensively in Mexican cooking. Pigs were first brought into the country by the Spanish in the sixteenth century, along with horses, cows, chickens, rice and wheat flour. In turn, the Spanish took tomatoes, chocolate, vanilla, corn, potatoes, many tropical fruits and, of course, chillies and sweet peppers back to Europe.

1 kg (2¼ lb) boneless pork neck or shoulder, cut into long strips
750 ml (1¼ pints) water
zest of one lemon
zest of one orange
4 spring onions, chopped
2 cloves garlic, crushed
2 fresh chillies, chopped
1.25 ml (¼ tsp) ground cumin
5 ml (1 tsp) salt

In a heavy casserole dish, arrange the pork strips in a single layer, adding barely enough water to cover. Add the zest of the lemon and orange, the onions, garlic, chillies, cumin and salt. Bring to the boil, then reduce the heat and simmer gently, covered, for about an hour, turning now and again, until the meat is fork tender. Remove the meat and allow it to cool.

When cool, shred the meat into bits by hand or by using a fork. Season to taste and reheat the meat mixture before serving.

SERVES 6

SEAFOOD FILLING

Mexico is a long, narrow country, bordered by oceans. A great variety of good seafood is readily available.

30 ml (2 tbsp) olive oil
1 medium onion, finely chopped
1 red pepper, seeds removed, finely chopped
2 cloves garlic, crushed
1 can (about 400 g/14 oz) Mexican-style tomatoes with chilli (see note on page 41)
400 g (14 oz) seafood mix, defrosted and drained (see note) or
400 g (14 oz) flaked, cooked fish
60 g (2 oz) feta cheese, crumbled
salt and freshly ground black pepper

GARNISH
fresh coriander leaves

NOTE: This mix usually consists of shrimps, squid and mussels.

Heat oil in a suitable saucepan. Stir in onion and red pepper and cook gently until softened. Stir in garlic and cook for barely a minute. Add tomatoes and cook, covered, for 20 minutes or until reduced and thickened. Stir in seafood mix (or flaked fish) and cook for about 5 minutes or until heated through. Add feta and stir until it starts to melt. Add seasoning to taste and garnish with coriander leaves.

SERVES 4

SEAFOOD FILLING (THIS PAGE) IN A CRISP TACO

MEXICAN CHICKEN

Not only is this recipe worth making in its own right, it is also a good way of making use of leftover cooked chicken, or smartening up a bought cooked chicken.

30 ml (2 tbsp) sunflower oil
1 medium onion, finely chopped
2 fresh green chillies, finely chopped
1 clove garlic, crushed
30 ml (2 tbsp) tomato paste
5 ml (1 tsp) ground cumin
30 ml (2 tbsp) chopped fresh
coriander leaves
500 g (18 oz) ripe, red tomatoes,
skinned, seeds removed, chopped
500 g (18 oz) cooked chicken,
shredded
salt and freshly ground black pepper

GARNISH
fresh coriander leaves

Heat the oil in a suitable saucepan and stir in the onion. Cook gently until softened, but not browned. Stir in the chillies and garlic and cook for 1–2 minutes. Stir in the tomato paste, cumin, coriander leaves, tomatoes and a little seasoning. Cover and simmer for 15 minutes or until reduced and thickened. Add the chicken and cook, uncovered, for another 5 minutes or until the chicken is hot and the sauce well reduced. Season to taste and then sprinkle with coriander leaves.
SERVES 4

PICADILLO

This is a very good variation of the basic chilli-beef filling. The combination of raisins, nuts and vinegar gives it a sweet-sour taste.

15 ml (1 tbsp) sunflower oil
1 medium onion, finely chopped
1 clove garlic, crushed
1 fresh, green chilli, finely chopped
500 g (18 oz) lean, minced beef
30 ml (2 tbsp) red wine vinegar
500 g (18 oz) ripe, red tomatoes,
skinned and chopped
30 ml (2 tbsp) tomato paste
45 g (1½ oz) seedless raisins
a pinch of ground cloves
5 ml (1 tsp) ground cinnamon
30 g (1 oz) flaked almonds,
lightly toasted
salt and freshly ground black pepper

Heat the oil in a suitable saucepan. Add the onion and cook gently until softened, but not browned. Stir in the garlic and chilli and cook, stirring, for 1–2 minutes. Stir in the minced beef and some seasoning. Increase the heat and stir-fry until the meat starts to brown. Add the vinegar, tomatoes, tomato paste, raisins and spices and simmer, uncovered, for approximately 20 minutes or until the mixture is reduced and thickened and the meat is tender. Now season to taste and stir in the almonds.
SERVES 4–6

REFRIED BEANS

They're named 'refried' as first the beans are boiled, then 'recooked' and mashed to a suitable consistency for a topping or side dish. Beans always appear on the Mexican table, either simply boiled and seasoned, or refried in a variety of ways.

500 g (18 oz) red or white beans
2 medium onions, finely chopped
3 cloves garlic, crushed
1 bay leaf
2–4 fresh chillies
90 ml (6 tbsp) sunflower oil
1–2 ripe, red tomatoes, skinned
and chopped
salt and freshly ground black pepper

Soak the beans overnight. Skim off any grit. Drain and place in a saucepan with enough water to cover. Add half the onion and half the garlic, the bay leaf and chillies. Cover and bring to the boil, then reduce the heat and simmer, adding more boiling water if necessary. When the beans start to soften, stir in 15 ml (1 tbsp) of the oil. Cook until soft, then stir in 15 ml (1 tbsp) salt and cook for 30 minutes or until very soft and almost all the liquid has evaporated. Stir now and again to prevent the beans sticking.

Heat 30 ml (2 tbsp) of the oil in a wide pan and add the remaining onion. Cook gently until very soft but not browned. Stir in the remaining garlic. Add the tomato and cook for another few minutes. Gradually stir in the beans with the remaining liquid, mashing them with the remaining oil. Cook, stirring, until it forms a dryish paste. Season to taste and add more chopped chillies if necessary.

Use as a vegetarian filling or as a topping. The mixture can be thinned down if necessary.
SERVES 6–8

SHREDDED PORK FILLING (PAGE 18) IN A TORTILLA, SERVED WITH SHREDDED LETTUCE, AND SALSA (THIS PAGE)

TACO TOPPINGS

A variety of high protein taco fillings – either beans or meat – served hot, are lightened with crunchy toppings of chopped fresh vegetables and chillies, known as 'salsas', which is the Spanish word for 'sauces'.

SALSA

250 g (9 oz) ripe, red tomatoes, skinned, seeds removed, chopped
4 spring onions, thinly sliced
15 ml (1 tbsp) chopped fresh coriander leaves
2 fresh chillies, seeds removed, chopped
15 ml (1 tbsp) red wine vinegar
salt and freshly ground black pepper

Mix all the ingredients together well, adding seasoning to taste.
SERVES 6

GUACAMOLE

Use this versatile mixture as a topping for a variety of tacos or as a dip for crisp taco chips. It also makes a very good sauce with grilled fish or chicken.

2 large, ripe avocados, coarsely chopped
15 ml (1 tbsp) lemon juice
4 spring onions, thinly sliced
1 ripe, red tomato, chopped
2 fresh chillies, chopped
30 ml (2 tbsp) chopped fresh coriander leaves
salt and freshly ground black pepper

Mix all the ingredients together well to a fairly coarse consistency and then simply season to taste.
SERVES 6

Soups & Salads

Chillies and spices intensify the flavours of chunky wholesome soups and bountiful salads. They make satisfying meals-in-one any day of the week. Put together a soup and a salad for robust suppers or super Sunday meals, adding crusty rolls or peasant-style breads for complete enjoyment.

FOR A WINTER SUNDAY SUPPER: *MOROCCAN-STYLE FISH SOUP* (PAGE 24) *SERVED WITH COUSCOUS AND HARISSA PASTE* (PAGE 8)

THAI-STYLE PUMPKIN & PRAWN SOUP

This soup has been slightly adapted from a typical Thai recipe. The base of coconut milk gives it an exquisite flavour. It's not difficult to prepare coconut milk in the home kitchen (see page 11), but blocks of creamed coconut and canned coconut milk are available today from oriental shops, which makes it even easier.

350 g (12 oz) pumpkin, peeled
and diced
15 ml (1 tbsp) lemon juice
125 g (4 oz) shelled prawns
2 spring onions, chopped
15 ml (1 tbsp) shrimp paste
(see page 11)
2 fresh chillies, sliced
750 ml (1¼ pints) thick
coconut milk
250 ml (8 fl oz) water
a grinding of pepper
60 g (2 oz) fresh basil leaves
Thai fish sauce (optional) (see note)
salt

NOTE: This is usually available from speciality oriental shops. If unobtainable, see Notes on Exotic Ingredients (page 11).

Sprinkle the pumpkin with the lemon juice and set aside.

Using a food processor, pound the prawns with the spring onions, shrimp paste and chillies, adding a little water if necessary, to form a thick paste. Pour half the coconut milk into a heavy saucepan. Add the pounded prawn paste and bring to the boil. Reduce the heat and stir until smooth. Add the pumpkin and cook gently for 10 minutes. Add the remaining coconut milk and the water. Add a grinding of pepper. Cover and simmer for 10 minutes or until the pumpkin is just tender, but not too soft.

Run a hand-held electric blender through the soup for 1–2 minutes to give it a good consistency. Most of the pumpkin pieces should still remain whole. Add the basil leaves and season to taste. Stir in some fish sauce if necessary. Serve hot.
SERVES 4–6

CHILLI CORN SOUP

A rich and creamy soup – redolent with the sweetness of fresh corn – is spiked with the bite of chillies. Try floating crisp taco chips on top, sprinkled with grated cheese, or add a spoonful of sharp salsa.

600 ml (1 pint) chicken stock
4 medium sweet corn,
kernels cut off the cob
1 bunch spring onions, thinly sliced
2 fresh chillies, finely chopped
30 g (1 oz) butter
10 ml (2 tsp) flour
125 ml (4 fl oz) single (thin) cream
salt and freshly ground black pepper

GARNISH
fresh coriander leaves

Heat the stock, add the corn and bring to the boil. Cook for about 5 minutes or until tender. Purée roughly, preferably with a hand-held electric blender if you have one, to maintain the texture.

In a suitable saucepan, melt the butter and cook the onions and chillies gently for a few minutes. Stir in the flour and cook for a further 1–2 minutes. Add the blended corn and stock, and heat. Pour in the cream and bring to a gentle simmer. Season to taste and strew with some fresh coriander leaves to garnish.
SERVES 4

SPICED LENTIL SOUP

Made from store cupboard ingredients, this thick, spicy soup is wonderfully comforting on a cold winter's night. The cumin and crisp onion topping are an added dimension that turns it into a special dish.

500 g (18 oz) red lentils
2 litres (3½ pints) water
5 ml (1 tsp) turmeric
1 can (about 400 g/14 oz) tomatoes
60 ml (4 tbsp) chopped fresh
coriander leaves
1 fresh chilli, finely chopped
75 g (2½ oz) cooked basmati rice
salt and freshly ground black pepper

30 ml (2 tbsp) sunflower oil
5 ml (1 tsp) cumin seeds
1 medium onion, thinly sliced

GARNISH
fresh coriander leaves

Soak the lentils for about 5 minutes, then drain and rinse well. Tip them into a saucepan and pour in the water. Bring to the boil, then add the turmeric. Reduce the heat and simmer, half covered, for 30 minutes. Purée, using a hand-held electric blender if you have one.

Now crush the tomatoes and add them together with the juice, the coriander, chilli and a little salt to taste. Bring to a simmer and cook, covered, for 15 minutes. Then stir in the rice and heat through. Season to taste.

Meanwhile, heat the oil and stir-fry the cumin briefly. Add the onion and fry, stirring often, until it is well browned and crisp. Lastly, sprinkle the onion over each plate of soup to garnish, together with a few fresh coriander leaves.

If the soup thickens on standing, thin it down using water or stock and adjust the seasoning.
SERVES 6–8

SPICY ORIENTAL FISH SOUP

The Western palate finds oriental tastes deliciously different. Once you get into the habit of Eastern flavour combinations, it becomes addictive. The healthy cooking methods are an added bonus.

500 g (18 oz) skinned firm white
fish fillets
2.5 ml (½ tsp) crushed fresh
root ginger
30 ml (2 tbsp) soy sauce
150 g (5 oz) rice noodles
or Chinese egg noodles
30 ml (2 tbsp) sunflower oil
1 bunch spring onions,
thinly sliced
1 clove garlic, crushed
5 ml (1 tsp) turmeric
1 fresh chilli, chopped
grated rind of a lemon
1.5 litres (2¾ pints) light fish stock
30 ml (2 tbsp) dry sherry
175 g (6 oz) shredded lettuce
60 g (2 oz) fresh bean sprouts
30 g (1 oz) fresh coriander leaves

soy sauce, chilli and sesame oils

Cut the fish into cubes, mix cubes with the ginger and soy sauce and refrigerate. Meanwhile, soak the rice noodles in warm water for about 20 minutes or cook the egg noodles according to package instructions.

Heat the sunflower oil in a saucepan and add the spring onion. Cook gently until softened but still pale. Stir in the garlic, turmeric, chilli and lemon rind, and cook gently for 1–2 minutes. Pour in the stock and bring to the boil. Add the fish, sherry, well-drained noodles, lettuce and bean sprouts. Cook for a minute or until the fish is opaque and just cooked through, taking care not to allow it to boil. Stir in the coriander leaves. Season to taste and serve. Pass round the soy sauce and oils at the table.

SERVES 4–6

SPICED MINCE, BEAN & NOODLE SOUP

This hearty meal of soup makes a cheering midweek meal. Serve it with warm tortillas or wedges of pitta bread. Follow up with fresh fruit and cheese, or a baked custardy pudding.

250 g (9 oz) dried haricot beans
1.5 litres (2¾ pints) water
3 medium carrots, scraped and sliced
2 medium onions, chopped
2 cloves garlic, crushed
1 kg (2¼ lb) tomatoes, skinned
and chopped
30 ml (2 tbsp) tomato paste
1 bay leaf
1 beef stock cube
500 g (18 oz) very lean minced steak
5 ml (1 tsp) chilli powder
(see page 9)
2.5 ml (½ tsp) ground cumin
1 extra large egg, beaten
60 ml (4 tbsp) water
125 g (4 oz) uncooked small
shell noodles
salt and freshly ground black pepper

Soak the beans overnight. When you are ready to use them, boil them rapidly for 10 minutes, then drain, discarding any water.

Place beans in a large saucepan with the water from the ingredients list. Bring to the boil and remove any scum. Add the carrots, onions, one crushed clove garlic, chopped tomatoes, tomato paste, bay leaf and freshly ground black pepper. Reduce the heat and simmer for about an hour. Stir in the crumbled stock cube. Combine the mince, spices, remaining crushed clove garlic, egg, 60 ml (4 tbsp) water, salt and pepper. Form into small balls and add to the soup. Simmer for 45 minutes. Add salt to taste and stir in the noodles. Cook until tender and adjust the seasoning if you think it necessary.

SERVES 4–6

MOROCCAN-STYLE FISH SOUP

Moroccan flavours are excellent. The charmoula, one of many popular variations, is the marinade used with fish. The marinated fish could simply be grilled or baked. Here it is made into a bountiful soup that forms the base of a splendid meal.

1 kg (2¼ lb) fresh line fish fillets

CHARMOULA
4 cloves garlic, crushed
15 ml (1 tbsp) ground cumin
15 ml (1 tbsp) paprika
2.5 ml (½ tsp) crushed, fresh chillies
60 ml (4 tbsp) chopped parsley
60 ml (4 tbsp) chopped fresh
coriander leaves
60 ml (4 tbsp) lemon juice
30 ml (2 tbsp) olive oil
5 ml (1 tsp) salt

FISH SOUP
60 ml (4 tbsp) olive oil
2 medium onions, chopped
4 sticks celery, finely chopped
6 cloves garlic, crushed
15 ml (1 tbsp) crushed fresh chillies
5 ml (1 tsp) ground cumin
15 ml (1 tbsp) paprika
2.5 ml (½ tsp) cinnamon
1 can (about 400 g/14 oz) chopped
tomatoes
1 litre (1¾ pints) fish stock
salt and freshly ground black pepper

hot couscous (see note on page 53)
harissa paste (see page 8)

Mix and blend the ingredients for the charmoula together thoroughly. Then cut the fish into fairly large pieces and rub well all over with the charmoula. Allow fish to marinate while you are preparing the soup.

To make the fish soup, heat the olive oil gently in a large saucepan. Add the onions and celery, and cook gently until softened but still pale in colour. Add the garlic, crushed chillies and spices. Stir together for 1–2 minutes until fragrant. Add the tomatoes and fish stock, and cook, uncovered, for approximately 15 minutes.

Now add the marinated fish pieces and cook gently for about another 5 minutes or until the fish is just cooked through. Season to taste and ladle into soup bowls over mounds of hot couscous. Pass round the harissa paste at the table.
SERVES 6

BROWN RICE & BLACK BEAN SALAD WITH SPICY DRESSING

Chock-full of contrasting tastes and textures, vegetarians will find this a most pleasing salad. Meat lovers can add some spicy sausage if they would like to – the Portuguese varieties, for instance, which are found at well-stocked delis and Portuguese grocers.

RICE
15 ml (1 tbsp) sunflower oil
1 small onion, finely chopped
475 g (17 oz) brown rice
750 ml (1¼ pints) vegetable or chicken stock

VEGETABLES
175 g (6 oz) corn kernels
175 g (6 oz) black beans, soaked, cooked and drained

DRESSING
60 ml (4 tbsp) red wine vinegar
150 ml (¼ pint) sunflower oil
1 clove garlic, crushed
5 ml (1 tsp) chilli sauce
salt and freshly ground black pepper

TO FRY
250 g (9 oz) spicy sausage, sliced (optional)

CHILLI CORN SOUP (PAGE 23) SERVED WITH SALSA (PAGE 21) AND NACHOS

GARNISH
1 large red pepper, finely chopped
1 avocado, peeled and chopped
1 bunch fresh coriander, well washed
baby lettuce leaves

thick soured cream

Heat the oil gently, add the onion and cook until pale golden. Stir in the rice and stock, and bring to a simmer. Cover and reduce the heat. Cook for 20 minutes. Add the corn and cook for a further 10 minutes or until the rice is tender and the liquid absorbed. Season to taste. Mix the ingredients for the dressing well. Now mix the beans and dressing into the corn and rice mixture. Stir-fry the sliced sausage if you are using it and add. Sprinkle with the chopped pepper, avocado and herbs. Tuck in baby lettuce leaves. When serving, pass round a bowl of thick soured cream.
SERVES 6

ROASTED VEGETABLE SALAD WITH CHILLI DRESSING

The roasting of vegetables for salads is very much in the style of Spanish cooking. You see its influence in Mexico, where vegetables are often roasted before being prepared in sauces.

2 medium red tomatoes
2 red peppers
2 yellow peppers
2 medium onions

DRESSING
1 fresh chilli, finely chopped
juice of half a lemon
125 ml (4 fl oz) olive oil
salt and freshly ground black pepper

Prick the vegetables all over, arrange them on a well-oiled baking tray and put into the oven at 230 °C (450 °F; gas 8). Remove the tomatoes after 5 minutes. Leave the peppers and onions for another 25 minutes or until blackened and tender. Wrap the peppers in a plastic bag until cool enough to handle, then peel off the skin, remove the seeds and chop. Peel the onions and chop. Skin the tomatoes and chop. Mix the ingredients for the dressing together well. Now mix all the chopped vegetables, pour the dressing over and season to taste. Serve as a starter with wedges of warm pitta bread.
SERVES 4–6

CURRIED BEEF & RICE SALAD

Rare beef in a gentle curry dressing goes perfectly in a rice-based salad, and the lentils add just the right touch of texture.

500 g (18 oz) rare-roasted beef, diced
250 g (9 oz) rice, freshly cooked
1 medium onion, finely chopped
250 g (9 oz) brown lentils, freshly cooked
1–2 medium carrots, cut in julienne strips
2 medium tomatoes, diced

CURRY DRESSING
250 ml (8 fl oz) sunflower oil
60 ml (4 tbsp) mango chutney
30 ml (2 tbsp) apple cider vinegar
juice of half a lemon
15 ml (1 tbsp) mild curry powder (see page 71)
salt and freshly ground black pepper

GARNISH
fresh coriander leaves

Place the salad ingredients in a suitable bowl. Mix the dressing ingredients together and season to taste. Pour into the salad bowl and mix gently. Add more seasoning if necessary and garnish generously with the coriander leaves.
SERVES 6

SPICED CHICKEN SALAD

Try serving the salad in fresh taco shells. The crispness of the taco is a delicious foil for the creaminess of the salad. First fill the taco shell with a bed of shredded lettuce, then top a serving of chicken salad with a spoonful of guacamole (see page 21).

500 g (18 oz) cooked, shredded chicken

DRESSING
125 ml (4 fl oz) soured cream
125 ml (4 fl oz) thick mayonnaise
5 ml (1 tsp) mild curry powder (see page 71)
1 clove garlic, crushed
salt and freshly ground black pepper
4–6 taco shells
125 g (4 oz) guacamole (see page 21)
baby lettuce leaves
1 firm, ripe avocado, peeled and sliced (optional)
lemon juice (optional)

GARNISH
baby red and yellow tomatoes

Mix the ingredients for the dressing together thoroughly. Now mix the chicken with the dressing and season to taste. Serve the salad as described in the introduction.

Alternatively, omit the tacos and simply serve the chicken salad on a bed of baby lettuce leaves. Add slices of avocado brushed with lemon juice to prevent browning.

In either case, garnish with baby red and yellow tomatoes and a few baby lettuce leaves.
SERVES 4–6

ROASTED VEGETABLE SALAD (PAGE 26), SPICY SAUSAGE AND CHICKEN LIVER PÂTÉ SALAD (THIS PAGE)

SPICY SAUSAGE & CHICKEN LIVER PÂTÉ SALAD

The base of this salad is a home-made sausage and chicken liver pâté. The richness of the pâté is balanced by the freshness of the green salad leaves.

500 g (18 oz) chicken livers
15 ml (1 tbsp) butter
15 ml (1 tbsp) oil
30 ml (2 tbsp) brandy
1 clove garlic, crushed
2 extra large eggs
125 ml (4 fl oz) single (thin) cream
125 g (4 oz) streaky bacon,
thinly sliced
150 g (5 oz) smoked, spicy sausage,
skinned and sliced
mixed green salad leaves for six

DRESSING
125 ml (4 fl oz) sunflower oil
45 ml (3 tbsp) apple cider vinegar
1.25 ml (¼ tsp) chilli sauce
1.25 ml (¼ tsp) prepared, hot mustard
15 ml (1 tbsp) soy sauce
15 ml (1 tbsp) chopped fresh
coriander leaves
1.25 ml (¼ tsp) ground coriander
salt and freshly ground black pepper

Trim the chicken livers and pat dry thoroughly using paper towels. Set aside 125 g (4 oz) of the livers. Heat the butter and oil, and brown the remaining chicken livers quickly over a high heat so that they are still pink inside. Remove using a slotted spoon and season.

Now pour the brandy into the pan. Add the garlic and allow to bubble furiously. Pour over the fried livers. Purée the reserved raw livers with the eggs, cream and seasoning. Now line a non-stick loaf tin (of about 20 x 10 x 6 cm or 8 x 4 x 2½ in) with the bacon. Pour in half the purée. Arrange a layer of fried livers, then a layer of sausage in the loaf tin. Then pour over the remaining purée. Stand the loaf tin on a baking tray (in case of spills) and bake at 160 °C (325 °F; gas 3) for about 45 minutes or until it has set. Allow the pâté to stand for 10 minutes before turning it out, while you mix the ingredients for the dressing together well.

To serve, divide the salad leaves among six plates. Top with thick slices of the warm pâté. Drench with the dressing and top with coriander leaves.

SERVES 6

SHREDDED CHICKEN WITH SPICED WALNUT SAUCE

In this Eastern European dish, the flavours of the nuts, spices and fresh herbs complement one another most beautifully.

1 chicken, about 1.5 kg (3½ lb)
1 litre (1¾ pints) water
3 medium onions
2–3 sprigs fresh parsley
2–3 sprigs fresh thyme
1 bay leaf
30 ml (2 tbsp) sunflower oil
100 g (3½ oz) walnuts,
lightly toasted
3 cloves garlic, crushed
2.5 ml (½ tsp) ground coriander
2.5 ml (½ tsp) cayenne pepper
1.25 ml (¼ tsp) ground cinnamon
1.25 ml (¼ tsp) turmeric
15 ml (1 tbsp) finely chopped
fresh mint
15 ml (1 tbsp) finely chopped parsley
5 ml (1 tsp) wine vinegar
salt and freshly ground black pepper

GARNISH
chopped fresh mint
chopped fresh parsley
baby lettuce leaves

Poach the chicken gently with the water, one of the onions (sliced), the parsley, thyme, bay leaf and seasoning to taste until tender. Allow to cool in the stock. Remove skin and bones, and shred the meat. Strain the stock and set aside. Heat the oil and cook the remaining onions (chopped) gently until soft. Grind the toasted walnuts in a processor, then stir into the onions along with the garlic. Pour in 250 ml (8 fl oz) of the reserved stock and simmer, uncovered, for about 15 minutes or until well reduced. If necessary, thin down with a little more stock. Stir in the spices, herbs and vinegar and cook for a few minutes. Season to taste. Mix the walnut sauce with the chicken and mound on a platter. Sprinkle with mint and parsley and surround with baby lettuce leaves. Chill for 1–2 hours before serving.
SERVES 6

THAI-STYLE BEEF SALAD

This delicious Thai salad uses mint and coriander leaves, contrasting the coolness of the fresh herbs with the spiciness of the chilli.

500 g (18 oz) fillet of beef
sunflower oil for moistening
3 cloves garlic, chopped
60 ml (4 tbsp) fresh mint leaves,
chopped
3 fresh red chillies, thinly sliced
(remove seeds and membrane
for a milder taste)
1–2 small onions, finely chopped
30 ml (2 tbsp) lemon juice
30 ml (2 tbsp) Thai fish sauce
(see page 11)
salt and pepper

lettuce leaves

GARNISH
1 tomato, cut into thin wedges
1 or 2 spring onions, thinly sliced
fresh coriander leaves

Moisten the piece of beef with sunflower oil and roast at 220 °C (425 °F; gas 7) for 15–20 minutes. Slice crosswise into thin strips and set aside. Pound together the garlic, mint, chillies, onions, lemon juice and fish sauce. Then mix this with the beef and adjust the seasoning if you think it necessary.

Serve the salad warm or at room temperature on a bed of lettuce leaves. Add some tomato slices and scatter over spring onions and coarsely shredded coriander leaves.
SERVES 4–6

THAI SQUID SALAD

This is an excellent calamari salad, spicy but fresh-tasting. The traditional Thai fish sauce gives it its distinctive flavour.

400 g (14 oz) squid (calamari),
cleaned and thinly sliced
30 ml (2 tbsp) Thai fish sauce
(see note)
60 ml (4 tbsp) lemon juice
10 ml (2 tsp) chilli sauce
1 medium onion, thinly sliced
in half-moons
1 tomato, thinly sliced in wedges
8 whole, fresh red chillies
a pinch of sugar (optional)
fresh coriander leaves

GARNISH
lettuce leaves (optional)

NOTE: This is usually available from speciality oriental shops. If unobtainable, see Notes on Exotic Ingredients (page 11).

Half-fill a saucepan with water and bring it to a simmer. Place the sliced squid (calamari) in a strainer and hold it in the simmering water for barely 2 minutes, by which time the squid should be opaque and tender. Remember that it is overcooking that toughens squid. Transfer to a bowl. Pour the fish sauce and lemon juice over and toss together. Mix in the chilli sauce. Add the onion, tomato and chillies, and a pinch of sugar only if necessary.

Sprinkle with coriander leaves and garnish with lettuce leaves if you would like to.
SERVES 4–6

FOR A THAI DINNER: *THAI-STYLE PUMPKIN AND PRAWN SOUP* (PAGE 23), *THAI GREEN CHICKEN CURRY* (PAGE 70),
THAI CUCUMBER SALAD (PAGE 66), *THAI-STYLE BEEF SALAD* (PAGE 28)

Pasta

Pasta is a perennial favourite, enjoyed from East to West. With added chilli and spice, the results are robust, satisfying and deliciously addictive. Some of these recipes are for traditional Italian dishes, others are popular oriental recipes. Many are lively contemporary dishes in the style of the innovative Californian chefs.

FOR A PASTA SUPPER: *GREEN SALAD WITH SALAMI; SMOKED CHICKEN AND CHILLI TAGLIATELLE (PAGE 32); PEARS AND PARMESAN*

SINGAPORE NOODLES

*All the different ingredients
add up to a tasty meal of a dish that's
enjoyed daily in Singapore.
You could use Chinese egg noodles
instead of the rice vermicelli
as a variation.*

200 g (7 oz) rice vermicelli
60 ml (4 tbsp) sunflower oil
I red pepper, cut into strips
200 g (7 oz) shelled shrimps
2 cloves garlic, crushed
2 fresh red chillies, finely chopped
300 g (11 oz) chicken breast fillets,
cut crosswise into strips
10 ml (2 tsp) ground cumin
5 ml (1 tsp) ground coriander
1.25 ml (¼ tsp) turmeric
175 ml (6 fl oz) chicken stock
6 spring onions, finely chopped
175 g (6 oz) bean sprouts
soy sauce
salt

Prepare the rice vermicelli according
to the manufacturer's instructions.
Drain well. Heat 15 ml (1 tbsp) of
the oil in a wide pan and add the
strips of pepper. Cook for about
5 minutes or until tender-crisp.
Remove using a slotted spoon.

Add a further 30 ml (2 tbsp) of
the oil to the pan. Now pat the
shrimps dry thoroughly using
paper towels and add. Stir-fry for
1–2 minutes until curled and pink.
Remove using a slotted spoon.

Pour in all the remaining oil.
Add the garlic, chillies, strips of
chicken, spices and salt. Stir-fry for
a few minutes – just until the
chicken is cooked through, then
remove using a slotted spoon

Now pour the stock into the pan
and add the vermicelli. Cook
together until thoroughly heated
through. Return the red pepper,
shrimps and chicken to the pan and
heat through. Mix in the onions
and bean sprouts. Add extra salt
and soy sauce to taste.
SERVES 4

CHILLI-GARLIC NOODLES

*These oriental noodles, good to eat
on their own, also make a zesty
accompaniment to a simple main
course of grilled chicken or steaks.*

250 g (9 oz) thin, fresh noodles
or dried vermicelli
30 ml (2 tbsp) sunflower oil
I fresh red chilli, finely chopped
2 cloves garlic, finely chopped
15 ml (1 tbsp) soy sauce
15 ml (1 tbsp) chicken stock
15 ml (1 tbsp) finely chopped
spring onion

Cook the noodles until just done.
Drain, then cover with warm water
to stop them sticking. Heat the oil
gently in a wok or large, heavy pan.
Add the chopped chilli and garlic,
and stir-fry for a few seconds. Stir in
the drained noodles and mix well.
Add the soy sauce, chicken stock
and spring onion. Toss again and
serve immediately.
SERVES 2–4

PASTA ARRABIATA

*The Italian word 'arrabiata' means
'enraged' or 'angry', which refers to
the heat of the chilli in the sauce.
Use penne or quill-shaped pasta
for added interest.*

I medium onion, very finely chopped
I clove garlic, crushed
I fresh, red chilli, split
125 g (4 oz) fatty bacon, finely
chopped
I can (about 400 g/14 oz) tomatoes,
crushed
400 g (14 oz) penne
salt and freshly ground black pepper

finely chopped parsley
grated Parmesan cheese

Cook the onion, garlic, chilli and
bacon gently in a suitable pan until
the onion is softened, but not
browned. Stir in the tomatoes and a
little salt. Cover and simmer for
20–30 minutes until the mixture is
reduced and thickened. Remove the
chilli and season to taste. Toss
together with the hot, drained pasta.
Sprinkle with parsley and pass
round the Parmesan.
SERVES 4

FUSILLI WITH SPICY RED PESTO

*Sun-dried tomatoes are usually
sold in jars, covered with oil
and flavoured with garlic and herbs.
Pound the whole lot together
for an instant sauce, spiking it with
chilli for extra zest.*

400 g (14 oz) fusilli

PESTO
250 g (9 oz) sun-dried tomatoes
in basil-flavoured oil
2 fresh red chillies, chopped
salt and freshly ground black pepper

freshly grated Parmesan cheese

Cook the pasta and drain, reserving
some of the cooking water.
Meanwhile purée the tomatoes,
together with the oil in which they
were supplied, to form a paste. Add
the chopped chillies and pound
together. Add salt and freshly
ground black pepper to taste. If the
mixture seems too thick, thin down
with some of the reserved cooking
water. Toss the pasta with the spicy
red pesto. Pass round the Parmesan.
SERVES 4

PASTA WITH SQUID & CHILLI CREAM SAUCE

This is an unusual squid (calamari) dish. The method of preparing the sauce is first class, and remember fast, fierce cooking will ensure tender squid. Use fresh squid, if at all possible. If you use tubes of baby squid, then simply halve; if using larger pieces, then cut into squares and score on the inside. Remember that if you're buying fresh squid, you'll need to ask for twice the amount to remain with 400 g (14 oz) once it's been cleaned.

375 ml (13 fl oz) boiling water
1 dried red chilli, chopped
1 medium onion, finely chopped
1 clove garlic, crushed
5 ml (1 tsp) ground coriander
1 red pepper, seeds removed, chopped
1 fresh red chilli, chopped
125 ml (4 fl oz) single (thin) cream
400 g (14 oz) cleaned squid (calamari)
olive oil for frying
salt

400 g (14 oz) short pasta

Pour the water over the dried chilli and leave to soak for approximately 30 minutes. Pour into a saucepan and add the onion, garlic, coriander, red pepper and fresh chilli. Simmer for about 20 minutes or until the vegetables are tender. Blend the mixture in a small food processor until smooth. Mix with the cream and reheat until the sauce has been reduced and slightly thickened. Add salt to taste. Cut the squid (calamari) tubes in half and score on the inside. Stir-fry over high heat in a wide, heavy pan in a minimum of oil until just cooked and curled. Mix the squid with the hot sauce and serve immediately with the drained, hot pasta.
SERVES 3–4

PORTUGUESE-STYLE MUSSEL PASTA

The Portuguese combine pork with seafood most successfully. Here I've used the combination in a sauce for pasta. It's delicious, and, of course, coriander is the herb which is used prolifically in Portuguese cooking.

125 g (4 oz) bacon
30 ml (2 tbsp) olive oil
1 large onion, finely chopped
3 cloves garlic, crushed
1 dried red chilli, seeds removed, chopped
500 g (18 oz) ripe, red tomatoes, skinned, seeds removed, chopped
250 ml (8 fl oz) dry white wine, or half mussel liquor (see note) and half wine
250 g (9 oz) spicy chorizo sausage, skinned and chopped
400 g (14 oz) steamed mussels, on the half-shell
salt and freshly ground black pepper

500 g (18 oz) pasta

GARNISH
fresh coriander leaves

NOTE: This refers to the liquid released from the mussels during the process of steaming.

Remove any rind and chop the bacon. Cook it gently in a saucepan until the fat runs. Add the oil and heat gently. Stir in the onion and cook until softened. Stir in the garlic and chilli. Add the tomatoes and wine, and bring to a bubble. Cook, uncovered, for 20–30 minutes or until reduced and thickened. Add the sausage and simmer for about 5 minutes, then add the mussels and allow to heat through. Season to taste and serve over any hot, freshly cooked pasta of your choice. Garnish with coriander leaves.
SERVES 4

SMOKED CHICKEN & CHILLI TAGLIATELLE

The sophistication of the sauce is very much in the style of Californian cuisine. It's an elegant dish, easy to make with pre-prepared smoked chicken breasts.

SAUCE
1 medium onion, finely chopped
1 medium carrot, finely chopped
1 stick celery, finely chopped
45 ml (3 tbsp) olive oil
3 fat cloves garlic
2 fresh, red chillies, chopped
1 fresh, red chilli, split
1 kg (2¼ lb) ripe, red tomatoes, skinned and chopped
15 ml (1 tbsp) tomato paste
350 g (12 oz) shredded, smoked chicken meat (reserve any skin)
250 ml (8 fl oz) single (thin) cream
salt and freshly ground black pepper

400 g (14 oz) tagliatelle

GARNISH
crisped chicken skin
fresh basil leaves

To make the sauce, cook the onion, carrot and celery gently in the olive oil until very soft, but still pale. Add a pinch of salt and a little water to prevent browning. Stir in 2 cloves of the garlic and the chopped chillies, then the tomatoes and tomato paste. Allow to simmer for 20–30 minutes or until reduced and thickened. Stir in the shredded chicken and add seasoning to taste. If you find it necessary, stir in a pinch of sugar.

In a separate container, heat the cream with the remaining crushed clove garlic and the split chilli. Toss with the hot drained pasta. To serve, crisp the chopped chicken skin (tiny pieces) in a hot pan. Top the creamy pasta with the chicken and tomato-chilli sauce.

Serve sprinkled with the crisp skin and basil leaves.
SERVES 4

CHILLI CHICKEN RAGOÛT WITH SPAGHETTI (THIS PAGE)

CHILLI CHICKEN RAGOÛT WITH SPAGHETTI

This is a lovely party dish. By the time you've skinned and boned the chicken thighs, there'll be a lot less meat, but still plenty to make a most generous sauce. The dark meat of the chicken is a very good choice, as it's flavourful and succulent.

2 kg (4½ lb) chicken thighs
30 ml (2 tbsp) olive oil
30 ml (2 tbsp) sunflower oil
2 medium onions, peeled
and chopped
3 sticks celery, chopped
2 medium carrots, scraped
and chopped
3 cloves garlic, crushed
3–4 fresh chillies, chopped
10 ml (2 tsp) dried oregano

1 bay leaf
30 ml (2 tbsp) tomato paste
500 ml (17 fl oz) dry red wine
1 litre (1¾ pints) chicken stock
45 g (1½ oz) unsalted butter
30 g (1 oz) flour
salt and freshly ground black pepper

500 g (18 oz) spaghetti

GARNISH
finely chopped parsley

Trim, wash and dry the chicken thighs. Mix the oils and heat in a heavy saucepan. Add the chicken and cook in batches until golden brown. Remove, using a slotted spoon, as the chicken becomes cooked and season lightly. Add the vegetables to the saucepan and cook very gently, stirring now and again, until softened. Stir in the garlic, chillies, oregano, bay leaf and the tomato paste. Return the chicken to the saucepan and pour in the wine and stock. Bring to a simmer, then reduce the heat and cook for 40 minutes or until tender. Strain and return the liquid to the saucepan. Bring to the boil and allow to reduce until lightly thickened. Mix the butter and flour together to form a paste. Whisk into the simmering liquid gradually and allow to cook until lightly thickened.

Once the chicken is cool enough to handle, skin and shred it into pieces, discarding the bones. Return to the sauce and allow to heat through and season to taste.

Serve the chilli chicken ragoût over freshly cooked spaghetti, garnished with a sprinkling of chopped parsley.

SERVES 6

SPAGHETTINI WITH BROCCOLI, ANCHOVY & CHILLI

This recipe describes one of my favourite Italian sauces – it offers an excellent combination of tastes and textures. Start with a tomato and mozzarella salad and finish with poached pears for a fine easy meal.

750 g (1¾ lb) broccoli
75 ml (2½ fl oz) olive oil
45 g (1½ oz) anchovies
2 cloves garlic, chopped
2 fresh red chillies, finely chopped

400 g (14 oz) spaghettini

Divide the broccoli into small florets and steam until tender. Heat the oil in a wide, heavy pan and add the anchovies and garlic, mashing them well with the oil. Stir in the finely chopped chillies, then the broccoli florets and mix together well.

Cook the spaghettini, drain and mix thoroughly with the sauce. Serve immediately.

SERVES 4

PASTA WITH MEXICAN-STYLE SAUCE

Mexicans do indeed eat pasta – the very fine angel's hair pasta in particular. If you can't get it, substitute vermicelli or spaghettini.

SAUCE
1 kg (2¼ lb) shoulder of pork, in one piece
750 ml (1¼ pints) water
4 cloves garlic
4 fresh chillies
2 cans (about 400 g/14 oz each) Mexican-style tomatoes with chilli (see note on page 41)
salt and freshly ground black pepper

400 g (14 oz) angel's hair pasta

Place pork in a heavy casserole dish. Pour over water. Add garlic, chillies and seasoning. Place a sheet of oiled, greaseproof paper directly on the surface. Cover tightly and bake at 160 °C (325 °F; gas 3) for 2–3 hours or until fork-tender. Remove meat from the oven and allow to cool in cooking liquid. Then remove and pull apart into long shreds by hand or by fork, returning shredded meat to cooking liquid. Use a slotted spoon to remove garlic and chillies. Add the tomatoes and cook over a high heat for 10 minutes, stirring often, or until slightly reduced. Season to taste and spoon the sauce over freshly cooked, drained pasta.

SERVES 6

RIGATONI WITH SPICY SAUSAGE, SPINACH & BLUE CHEESE

A rich and rugged sauce in the Italian style, it needs a fresh green salad to offset it and fruit to follow.

SAUCE
250 g (9 oz) spicy sausage
60 ml (4 tbsp) olive oil
250 g (9 oz) open, brown mushrooms, sliced
250 g (9 oz) spinach, well washed and coarsely shredded
2 cloves garlic, crushed
500 ml (17 fl oz) single (thin) cream
100 g (3½ oz) blue cheese, crumbled
10 ml (2 tsp) mustard seeds
salt and freshly ground black pepper

400 g (14 oz) rigatoni

If necessary, skin the sausage before slicing. Heat the oil in a wide, heavy pan. Add the sausage and stir-fry for about 5 minutes. Remove using a slotted spoon and set aside.

Add the sliced mushrooms to the pan and stir-fry for a few minutes. Add the shredded spinach and stir-fry until wilted. Now also stir in the garlic. Add the cream and cheese, and allow to simmer together, stirring now and again, for about 5–10 minutes or until reduced and slightly thickened.

Lastly, stir in the mustard seeds and sausage and allow to heat through thoroughly. Season to taste and toss the sauce with the freshly cooked, drained pasta.

SERVES 4–6

SPANISH SHRIMPS IN SPICY TOMATO SAUCE (PAGE 13), PORTUGUESE-STYLE MUSSEL PASTA (PAGE 32)

Fish & Seafood

Too many bland recipes have made fish unpopular, but here's a cache of spicy fish dishes guaranteed to catch compliments from both family and friends. Fish is an excellent choice if you are considering nutritional value. White fish is high in nutrients; low in calories. Research shows that the fatty acids contained in fish help to clear cholesterol from the system.

FOR A SEAFOOD BUFFET: *BAKED WHOLE FISH WITH BOUILLABAISSE SAUCE (PAGE 40) SERVED WITH GARLIC TOAST TRIANGLES (PAGE 40) AND ROUILLE (PAGE 41)*

Fish is cooked when it turns from translucent to opaque. Be careful not to overcook, as fish is most delicious when just firm and still moist.

PICKLED FISH

A traditional South African dish from the Cape. The spices tell of the Malay origins, for slaves were brought to the Cape by the Dutch settlers from their colony in the East.

1 kg (2¼ lb) sliced Cape salmon
or hake
salt and pepper
flour for coating
2 extra large eggs, beaten
sunflower oil for frying

SAUCE
3 medium onions, thinly sliced
15 ml (1 tbsp) sunflower oil
15 ml (1 tbsp) curry powder
(see page 71)
5 ml (1 tsp) turmeric
375 ml (13 fl oz) brown vinegar
125 ml (4 fl oz) water
30 g (1 oz) brown sugar
3 bay leaves
8 peppercorns
6 whole allspice

Season the fish with salt and pepper. Dip in flour and beaten egg and shallow- or deep-fry in hot oil until golden. Drain on crumpled brown paper and place in a heatproof bowl.

To make the sauce, fry the onions in the oil until golden. Stir in the curry powder and turmeric and cook, stirring, for 1–2 minutes. Add the vinegar, water, sugar, bay leaves, peppercorns and allspice. Bring to the boil, then reduce the heat and simmer until the onions are tender. Pour the hot mixture over the fried fish.

Allow fish to cool and refrigerate for a few days before serving.
SERVES 4–6

SPICED FISH WITH YOGHURT

This delicately spiced fish dish, Indian in origin, complements the fragrant Basmati Rice (see right) prepared in the pilaf manner.

500 g (18 oz) skinned and filleted fish
1.25 ml (¼ tsp) turmeric
1 medium onion, roughly chopped
2 medium onions, finely chopped
4 cloves garlic, crushed
125 ml (4 fl oz) plain yoghurt
1.25 ml (¼ tsp) cayenne pepper
a pinch of sugar
30 ml (2 tbsp) sunflower oil
6 whole cardamom pods
2 sticks (about 4 cm/1½ in each)
cinnamon
salt and freshly ground black pepper

Wash the fish and pat dry using paper towels. Cut into chunks and rub with the turmeric and some salt.

In a blender or food processor, make a thin paste of the roughly chopped onion, the garlic, yoghurt, cayenne, sugar, 2.5 ml (½ tsp) salt and a few grindings of black pepper. Heat the oil and sauté the fish gently, stirring all the time, for a few minutes without browning. Remove and set aside. Now sauté the finely chopped onion, adding more oil if necessary, together with the cardamom and cinnamon. Cook gently, while stirring, until golden. Reduce the heat to very low and add the yoghurt paste. Simmer very gently (without boiling) for approximately 5 minutes, stirring occasionally. Stir in the reserved fish and cook very gently, covered, for another 5 minutes or until very hot and cooked through.

Season to taste and serve on a bed of Spiced Basmati Rice (see next column) and accompanied by a salad of shredded lettuce, sliced tomato and fresh coriander leaves or with a chilled Tomato and Chilli Salad (see right).
SERVES 3–4

SPICED BASMATI RICE

200 g (7 oz) basmati rice
30 g (1 oz) butter
15 ml (1 tbsp) sunflower oil
4 whole cardamom pods
1 whole clove
2 sticks (about 4 cm/1½ in each)
cinnamon
500 ml (17 fl oz) water
5 ml (1 tsp) salt

Rinse the rice very well, then cover with water and leave to soak for 30 minutes. Drain and rinse again. Heat the butter and oil. First stir in the spices, then add the rice and stir for about a minute. Pour in the water and add the salt. Bring to the boil, cover and reduce the heat to very low. Simmer for 20 minutes. Uncover and fluff the rice with a fork. Then cover the rice again and cook for another 10 minutes or until the rice is tender. Serve with Spiced Fish with Yoghurt (see left).
SERVES 4

TOMATO & CHILLI SALAD

A chilled spicy tomato and chilli salad makes a good accompaniment to a spiced dish.

500 g firm, ripe tomatoes
1 small onion, thinly sliced
3 tablespoons sunflower oil
1 tbsp wine vinegar
salt
freshly ground black pepper
1 red chilli, chopped
1 clove garlic, crushed

Slice the tomatoes and place in a shallow bowl. Add the onion. Mix together oil, vinegar, salt, pepper, chilli and garlic to taste. Pour over the tomatoes. Serve chilled, with Spiced Fish with Yoghurt (see left).
SERVES 4–6

CALIFORNIAN GRILLED FISH WITH CHILLI-CORIANDER PESTO

This is an excellent way of preparing fish. It's contemporary, stylish and very much what Californian cuisine is all about – always innovative in twisting the traditional into new forms. Here a classic pesto uses fresh coriander leaves instead of basil, and chilli to hot it up.

PESTO
4 fresh, hot, green chillies, chopped
3 cloves garlic, crushed
30 g (1 oz) walnuts, chopped
30 g (1 oz) freshly grated Parmesan cheese
30 g (1 oz) fresh coriander leaves
125 ml (4 fl oz) olive oil
salt and freshly ground black pepper

4 fish steaks, about 1 kg (2¼ lb)
(use fresh line fish if obtainable)
olive oil

To make the pesto, place all the chillies, garlic, walnuts, Parmesan cheese and coriander leaves in a food processor and pound to a paste. Beat in the oil gradually and add a little seasoning to taste.

Slash the fish steaks diagonally two or three times, season and brush with oil. Slide under a pre-heated grill and cook for about 4 minutes on each side until browned and just cooked through. Spread with a spoonful of the pesto and cook for a further minute under the grill. Pass round the remaining pesto and serve with baked potatoes and a tomato salad.

SERVES 4

GRILLED FISH WITH TOMATO-CHILLI SAUCE, CORN & AVOCADO

Another recipe in the style of Californian cooking, this dish is remarkably successful with its contrasting tastes and textures.

4 portions fresh fish,
approximately 1 kg (2¼ lb) in total
(use fresh line fish if obtainable)
60 g (2 oz) butter, melted
1 clove garlic, crushed
30 ml (2 tbsp) chopped fresh coriander

SAUCE
500 g (18 oz) ripe, red tomatoes, skinned and chopped
5 ml (1 tsp) chilli paste
(see pages 8–9)
30 ml (2 tbsp) single (thin) cream
salt and freshly ground black pepper

1 firm, ripe avocado, cut into slices
250 g (9 oz) baby corn, steamed
fresh coriander leaves
wedges of lemon

Rinse the fish, pat dry using paper towels and season. Melt the butter and stir in the garlic and chopped coriander. Pour over the fish and slide under a hot grill. Grill each side until opaque and firm to the touch. Serve immediately.

To make the sauce, turn the tomatoes and chilli paste into a suitable saucepan. Reduce over a high heat until thick, then pour in the cream and bring the sauce to the boil. Season to taste.

Serve the fish without delay with the sauce, room temperature avocado, hot corn, coriander leaves and wedges of lemon.

SERVES 4

SPICY THAI SEAFOOD RICE

Restaurants specializing in seafood appear all along the coast of Thailand. Its sultry climate makes outdoor eating a way of life, and these eating places jut out right over the water. This deliciously spicy rice dish could form part of a seafood feast, or could make a casual meal on its own.

400 g (14 oz) seafood mix, thawed
(see note 1)
3 cloves garlic, chopped
5 ml (1 tsp) salt
1 small onion, finely chopped
3 fresh red chillies, chopped
45 ml (3 tbsp) sunflower oil
200 g (7 oz) freshly cooked Thai rice
(see note 2)
5 ml (1 tsp) sugar
15 ml (1 tbsp) soy sauce
15 ml (1 tbsp) Thai fish sauce
(see page 11)
30 g (1 oz) fresh basil leaves

GARNISH
fresh basil leaves

NOTE 1: This mix usually consists of shrimps, squid and mussels.

NOTE 2: Thai rice is available from most supermarkets.

Blanch the seafood mix briefly by dropping the pieces into boiling water. Wait for the water to return to the boil, then remove the seafood and drain thoroughly.

Pound the garlic, salt, onion and chillies to form a paste. Heat the oil in a heavy saucepan and brown the garlic mixture gently. Stir in the cooked rice. Add the seafood and cook, stirring constantly, until heated through. Stir in the sugar, soy sauce, fish sauce and basil leaves and cook for about a minute. Pack into a small bowl, then unmould onto a plate.

SERVES 4–6

CARIBBEAN-STYLE CURRIED FISH

Mildly spiced and creamy – this is the mark of a great deal of Caribbean cooking. Take note of the cooking technique, as it works well.

1 kg (2¼ lb) firm white fish fillets
75 ml (2½ fl oz) sunflower oil
1 medium onion, finely chopped
2 cloves garlic, crushed
2.5 ml (½ tsp) black mustard seeds
4 whole cloves
10 coriander seeds
1.25 ml (¼ tsp) cayenne pepper
15 ml (1 tbsp) curry powder
500 ml (17 fl oz) fish stock
175 ml (6 fl oz) single (thin) cream
a pinch of sugar
5 ml (1 tsp) lemon juice
salt and freshly ground black pepper

Wash and dry the fish fillets. Set aside. Heat the oil and fry the onion gently until softened. Stir in the garlic and spices and cook, stirring, for a minute or so. Pour in the stock and simmer for about 5 minutes. Add the cream and cook gently for another 5 minutes. Season to taste. Add the fillets of fish and turn off the heat. Allow to stand, covered, for about 30 minutes. Add the sugar and lemon juice. Season to taste and check the sweet-sour balance. Serve warm with boiled rice.
SERVES 4

CARIBBEAN-STYLE CURRIED FISH (THIS PAGE)

BAKED SPICED FISH

This easy Indian spiced fish dish is very good. Serve it simply with boiled rice, to set off the flavours.

1–1.5 kg (2¼–3½ lb) firm fish fillets, in one or two whole pieces
60 ml (4 tbsp) oil
4 medium onions, chopped
4 cloves garlic, crushed
2.5 ml (½ tsp) ground fennel
a chunk (about 2 cm/¾ in) of fresh root ginger, peeled and crushed
2.5 ml (½ tsp) cayenne pepper
2.5 ml (½ tsp) turmeric
2.5 ml (½ tsp) garam masala (see page 65)
30 ml (2 tbsp) lemon juice
3 sticks (about 4 cm/1½ in each) cinnamon
6 cardamom seeds
4 cloves
30 g (1 oz) chopped, fresh coriander leaves
salt and freshly ground black pepper

Wash the fish fillets and pat dry using paper towels. Make diagonal slashes across the fish. Place on an oiled, ovenproof dish and season lightly with salt and pepper. Heat the oil and sauté the onions, garlic and ginger gently until softened and lightly browned. Stir in the fennel, cayenne pepper, turmeric, garam masala, lemon juice, cinnamon sticks, cardamom, cloves, half the coriander and stir together for a few minutes. Then spread the mixture evenly over the fish.

Cover the fish with foil and bake at 180 °C (350 °F; gas 4) for about 30 minutes or until the fish is opaque and feels firm when pressed. To garnish, sprinkle with the remaining coriander.
SERVES 6

CALIFORNIAN GRILLED FISH WITH CHILLI-CORIANDER PESTO (PAGE 38)

Season the cleaned, trimmed fish and place in a well-oiled baking tin just large enough to hold it. Heat the oil and soften the onion, leeks and carrots gently, stirring often. Now add the garlic, tomatoes, tomato paste, bay leaf, dill, parsley, thyme, saffron and peel. Cook together for about 10 minutes, then add the wine and cook the mixture gently for another 5–10 minutes. Season to taste and pour the sauce inside and over the fish. Bake at 180 °C (350 °F; gas 4), basting now and again, for 45–60 minutes or until the fish is firm to the touch and flakes easily.

If you are using mussels, soak them well in cold water, then scrub and scrape off the beards. Discard any mussels that are not tightly closed and steam them on the hob, covered, with 125 ml (4 fl oz) wine for about 5 minutes. Discard any mussels that have not opened.

For serving, carefully lift the fish onto a long platter. If you have chosen to use mussels, add them now using a slotted spoon. Season the sauce to taste and pour it over the fish. Sprinkle with parsley and surround the fish with Garlic Toast Triangles (see below). Serve Rouille Sauce (see page 41) separately.
SERVES 6–8

BAKED WHOLE FISH WITH BOUILLABAISSE SAUCE

The flavours of the south of France that permeate this dish make it a perfect way of preparing a whole fish, and a very good reason for throwing a dinner party for friends. Serve it with a spicy rouille (see page 41) for added interest.

1 whole line fish, 2–2.5 kg
(4½–5 lb)
60 ml (4 tbsp) olive oil
1 medium onion, chopped
2 medium leeks, thinly sliced
2 medium carrots, finely chopped
2 cloves garlic, crushed
1 kg (2¼ lb) ripe, red tomatoes, skinned and chopped
1 small can (about 125 g/4 oz) tomato paste
1 bay leaf
15 ml (1 tbsp) chopped fresh dill
30 ml (2 tbsp) chopped parsley
a few sprigs of fresh thyme
a few saffron threads
a twist of orange peel
250 ml (8 fl oz) dry white wine
18 fresh mussels (optional)
125 ml (4 fl oz) dry white wine (optional)
salt and freshly ground black pepper

chopped parsley

GARLIC TOAST TRIANGLES

12 thick slices of white bread
olive oil for brushing
3 cloves garlic, crushed

Trim the crusts and slice the bread from corner to corner. Brush with olive oil and smear with crushed garlic. Bake at 180 °C (350 °F; gas 4) for about 20 minutes or until dried out and lightly browned.

Serve with Baked Whole Fish with Bouillabaisse Sauce (see left).
SERVES 6–8

ROUILLE

Rouille is a thick, home-made mayonnaise, spicy with chilli and Tabasco.

1 egg yolk
10 ml (2 tsp) chilli paste
(see pages 8–9)
5 ml (1 tsp) Dijon mustard
3 cloves garlic, crushed
15 ml (1 tbsp) lemon juice
125 ml (4 fl oz) olive oil
125 ml (4 fl oz) sunflower oil
Tabasco sauce
salt and freshly ground black pepper

In a food processor, whizz the egg yolk with the chilli paste, mustard and garlic. Gradually beat in lemon juice and oils to form a thick mayonnaise. Beat in Tabasco sauce to taste, drop by drop. Season to taste.

FISH BOBOTIE

The Malay slaves from the Dutch East Indies introduced the bobotie to the Dutch settlers in South Africa. Most often made with meat, the treatment is right with fish, resulting in a gentle, comforting dish.

1 kg (2¼ lb) steamed fish (you may
prefer either cod or hake)
2 medium onions, thinly sliced
30 g (1 oz) butter
2 slices white bread
300 ml (½ pint) buttermilk
3 extra large eggs
60 ml (4 tbsp) finely chopped
dried apricots
1 apple, peeled and grated
60 ml (4 tbsp) seedless raisins
30 ml (2 tbsp) sugar
15 ml (1 tbsp) mild curry powder
(see page 71)
30 ml (2 tbsp) lemon juice
salt and freshly ground black pepper
1.25 ml (¼ tsp) turmeric
6 fresh bay leaves

Drain the fish and flake. Melt the butter and sauté the onion until golden. Add the fish and stir for 1–2 minutes. Trim the crusts from the bread and cube. Mash with 60 ml (4 tbsp) of the buttermilk and 1 egg. Mix with the apricots, apple, raisins, sugar, curry powder, lemon juice, salt and pepper and fish. Season to taste. Turn the mixture into a buttered ovenproof dish, pressing the leaves into the top. Bake, uncovered, at 180 °C (350 °F; gas 4) for 15 minutes. Beat the remaining eggs with the remaining buttermilk and the turmeric and pour over the fish. Bake for another 20 minutes until the topping is set. Serve accompanied by steamed rice, chutney and a sambal of chopped tomato and onion with a dash of vinegar and some chopped chilli.
SERVES 6

NOTE ON CANNED MEXICAN-STYLE TOMATOES

If canned Mexican-style tomatoes are unobtainable, you could use any canned tomato and chilli mix or prepare your own using this recipe.

15 ml (1 tbsp) oil
1 small onion, chopped
5 ml (1 tsp) ground cumin
5 ml (1 tsp) chilli powder
(see page 9)
2 cloves garlic, crushed
1 can (about 400g/14 oz) tomatoes,
crushed
5 ml (1 tsp) dried, crushed oregano
salt and freshly ground black pepper

Heat the oil and soften the onion gently. Stir in the cumin, chilli powder and garlic. Add the tomatoes and oregano and simmer for 10–15 minutes. Add seasoning to taste and blend all the ingredients together roughly.

MEXICAN-STYLE BARBECUED FISH

Fresh coriander is the herb of Mexico. It gives a characteristic aroma that blends beautifully with the mix of tomato and orange that is favoured on the Veracruz coast.

1.5 kg (3½ lb) red roman
or red snapper, cleaned, with head
and tail left intact
1 bunch fresh coriander, chopped
1 medium onion, thinly sliced
75 ml (2½ fl oz) olive oil
125 ml (4 fl oz) orange juice
salt and freshly ground black pepper

SAUCE
1 can (about 400 g/14 oz) Mexican-
style tomatoes with chilli
(see note on this page)
45 ml (3 tbsp) chopped, stuffed olives
5 ml (1 tsp) dried oregano

GARNISH
shredded lettuce
fresh coriander leaves

Score the fish three times on each side. Season lightly with salt and pepper and place the coriander and onion inside. Rub the oil all over the fish and place in a baking tin. Pour over the orange juice. If convenient, allow fish to marinate for a few hours at room temperature or overnight in the refrigerator.

Grill the fish over hot coals until the skin is crisp and golden and flesh is opaque and firm to the touch. Alternatively, roast the fish, uncovered, at 230 °C (450 °F; gas 8) for 25 minutes or until the skin is starting to catch and just cooked through. To make the sauce, simmer all the ingredients together until heated through. When the fish is cooked, transfer to a warm serving dish and pour over the sauce. Garnish with shredded lettuce and fresh coriander. Serve with warm tortillas or steamed rice.
SERVES 4–6

SPICY MUSSELS

Mussels spiced with chilli work well and are reminiscent of the kind of dishes you may find in Portugal. Serving them with a risotto is unusual, but very good.

30 ml (2 tbsp) olive oil
1 small onion, finely chopped
250 ml (8 fl oz) dry white wine
1 ripe, red tomato, skinned, seeds removed, chopped
1 clove garlic, crushed
1 dried, red chilli, soaked, seeds removed, chopped
300 g (11 oz) shelled mussels, blanched
salt and freshly ground black pepper

GARNISH
fresh basil or coriander leaves

In a large, heavy pan, heat the olive oil. Add the onion and cook gently until soft, but still pale. Increase the heat and add the wine, tomato, garlic and chilli and cook until the liquid is reduced by half. Add the mussels and allow to heat through. Season to taste and garnish with basil or coriander leaves and serve with the Risotto (see next column).
SERVES 4

RISOTTO

30 g (1 oz) unsalted butter
15 ml (1 tbsp) olive oil
1 small onion, finely chopped
1 clove garlic, crushed
125 ml (4 fl oz) dry white wine
250 ml (8 fl oz) short-grain rice
1.25 litres (2¼ pints) vegetable or fish stock
salt and freshly ground black pepper

In a shallow, heavy pan, heat the butter and oil. Stir in the onion and cook gently until softened, but still pale. Add the garlic and wine and reduce over a high heat to a few spoonfuls. Now stir in the rice and 250 ml (8 fl oz) of the stock. Cook for about 20 minutes, stirring often, until all the stock is absorbed. If necessary, pour in more stock and continue to cook for approximately 20 minutes. Add seasoning to taste.
SERVES 4

ROASTED PRAWNS WITH PIRI-PIRI SAUCE

This is an easy way to deal with prawns, particularly if you need to cook lots of them. The method and timing stay the same; simply use a larger pan or several pans on separate shelves of the oven. Take care to arrange the prawns in a single layer so that they can cook evenly.

500 g (18 oz) large prawns, deveined
125 g (4 oz) butter
5 ml (1 tsp) chilli paste (see page 8)
15 ml (1 tbsp) chopped parsley
2.5 ml (½ tsp) dried oregano
3 cloves garlic, crushed
15 ml (1 tbsp) lemon juice
salt and freshly ground black pepper
Tabasco sauce (optional)

Heat the oven to 230 °C (450 °F; gas 8). Rinse the prawns and pat dry using paper towels. Cut up the butter and place in a roasting pan just large enough to take the prawns in a single layer. Melt the butter in the heated oven. Add the prawns and roast for 5 minutes. Turn the prawns and mix in the chilli paste, herbs, garlic and lemon juice. Roast for another 5 minutes or until the prawns are pink and curled. Add seasoning to taste and Tabasco sauce if you like it hotter. Serve with steamed rice or fresh, crusty bread.

Follow the prawns with a large mixed salad tossed in an olive oil and lemon juice dressing.
SERVES 3–4

Chicken

Chicken is much favoured today, as it is such a good-tasting, healthy food that lends itself to a myriad variations. These recipes are deliciously spicy innovations or unusual ethnic dishes to include in your menus for weekday eating or weekend feasting.

THE IBERIAN WAY: *PORTUGUESE PIRI-PIRI CHICKEN, SERVED WITH SPANISH RICE (BOTH PAGE 50)*

It is important never to overcook chicken. Take care to follow the touch test – chicken should always feel firm but springy, and taste beautifully moist and tender.

SPICED CHICKEN

The amount of spices in this dish is small enough not to intimidate the family, yet interesting enough to impress friends at dinner.

1 chicken (about 1 kg/2¼ lb),
cut into small portions
5 ml (1 tsp) turmeric
5 ml (1 tsp) chicken masala
30 ml (2 tbsp) sunflower oil
2 medium onions, finely chopped
3 potatoes, peeled and diced
3 cloves garlic, crushed
a chunk (about 2 cm/¾ in) of fresh
root ginger, peeled and crushed
1 fresh, green chilli, seeds removed,
chopped
3 cardamom pods, cracked
1 whole clove
2 sticks (about 4 cm/1½ in each)
cinnamon
1 ripe, red tomato
250 ml (8 fl oz) water
salt and freshly ground black pepper

GARNISH
fresh coriander leaves

Rub the chicken pieces with the turmeric, masala and seasoning and allow to stand for 30 minutes. Heat the oil and fry the onion gently until soft and pale golden. Now add the potatoes and a little more oil if necessary. Stir until very lightly browned. Season lightly and stir in the garlic and ginger. Stir in the chicken and cook until it has a good colour. If needed, add a little water to prevent catching. Add the chilli and the remaining spices. Cut the tomato in half and grate directly into the pot, discarding the skin. Add the water and bring to a simmer. Cover tightly and simmer gently for about 45 minutes or until very tender. Season to taste. To serve, sprinkle with a little Garam Masala (see page 65) and fresh coriander leaves and spoon onto a bed of Spiced Basmati Rice (see page 37).
SERVES 4

SPICED CHICKEN (THIS PAGE) SERVED WITH SPICED BASMATI RICE (PAGE 37)

CHICKEN & SAUSAGE JAMBALAYA

A Cajun meal-in-one, this is a down-to-earth, vigorous dish that needs only a green salad and fresh fruit to round it off.

1 medium chicken, cut into
small portions
60 ml (4 tbsp) sunflower oil
1 large onion, chopped
1 green pepper, chopped
3 sticks celery, chopped
3 cloves garlic, crushed
1 can (about 400 g/14 oz) tomatoes,
crushed
1 bay leaf
a few sprigs thyme
750 ml (1¼ pints) chicken stock
250 g (9 oz) spicy sausage,
skin removed, chopped
400 g (14 oz) long-grain rice
5 ml (1 tsp) cayenne pepper
salt and freshly ground black pepper
Tabasco sauce (optional)

GARNISH
chopped parsley

Wash the chicken pieces and pat dry using paper towels. Heat the oil in a heavy saucepan and brown the chicken. Remove using a slotted spoon. Add the onion, green pepper and celery to the saucepan and cook gently until the vegetables are soft, but the onion is still pale. Then stir in the garlic, crushed tomatoes with the juice, bay leaf, thyme, chicken stock and sausage.

Now return the chicken pieces to the saucepan. Bring to a simmer and cook for about 20 minutes.

Stir in the rice, 5 ml (1 tsp) salt and cayenne pepper. Cover and cook gently for about 30 minutes or until the chicken and the rice are tender and the liquid has been absorbed. Season to taste and add a dash of Tabasco if needed.

Sprinkle with chopped parsley to garnish and serve immediately.
SERVES 4–6

SPICED FRIED CHICKEN

The combination of spice and corn evokes the call of Africa. Yet this dish would also feel at home in Texas.

12 chicken portions
60 g (2 oz) yellow corn meal
(or maize meal)
5 ml (1 tsp) chilli powder
(see page 9)
5 ml (1 tsp) ground cumin
5 ml (1 tsp) ground coriander
5 ml (1 tsp) salt
oil for frying

Trim the chicken, rinse and pat dry. Season lightly. Mix the corn meal with the spices and use to coat the chicken pieces evenly on both sides. Deep-fry or shallow-fry on both sides in the hot oil until golden brown, then arrange in a single layer, skin side up, on the rack of a grill pan lightly brushed with oil. Complete the cooking in the oven at 240 °C (475 °F; gas 9) for about 15 minutes. Serve with a slightly sweet Braised Corn (see below).
SERVES 6–8

BRAISED CORN

45 g (1½ oz) butter
1 bunch spring onions, thinly sliced
2 red peppers, thinly sliced
1 clove garlic, crushed
3 ripe tomatoes, skinned
and chopped
1 fresh, red chilli, chopped
a pinch of sugar
350 g (12 oz) fresh sweetcorn kernels
125 ml (4 fl oz) chicken stock
30 ml (2 tbsp) chopped parsley
30 ml (2 tbsp) chopped fresh
coriander leaves
salt and freshly ground black pepper

Melt 30 g (1 oz) of the butter and add the spring onions and peppers. Cook gently until softened. Stir in

the garlic, tomatoes, chilli and sugar and cook for another 5 minutes. Add the sweetcorn, stock, parsley and seasoning. Simmer, uncovered, for 15 minutes or until the sweetcorn is tender. Stir in the remaining butter and the coriander leaves. Season to taste.
SERVES 6

SPICY GRILLED CHICKEN

A good way of cooking chicken on a barbecue, this light dish has the advantage of being low in calories, but interesting in its flavouring.

8 chicken breast portions, skinned
and filleted

MARINADE
2 cloves garlic, crushed
a chunk (about 2 cm/¾ in) of fresh
root ginger, peeled and crushed
2 fresh green chillies
10 ml (2 tsp) ground coriander
60 ml (4 tbsp) vinegar
60 ml (4 tbsp) sunflower oil
salt and freshly ground black pepper

GARNISH
fresh coriander leaves

Slash the chicken pieces crosswise two or three times and arrange in a single layer in a shallow dish. Blend the ingredients for the marinade well and pour the marinade over the chicken. Cover and leave to stand overnight in the refrigerator or for an hour at room temperature. Cook the chicken for a few minutes on each side, either under a preheated grill or over medium to hot coals until browned, but still moist.

Sprinkle with fresh coriander and serve with Coconut Rice (see page 61) and a cucumber and yoghurt salad (see page 63).
SERVES 4–6

SPICY CHICKEN PIE WITH CORN MEAL PASTRY

This corn meal (or maize meal) pastry is exceptionally good and can be used with a variety of fillings. Any spicy mince mixture encased in a turnover of the pastry would make a terrific pie. However, this spicy chicken filling is one that I can strongly recommend, as it admirably complements the delicious crust.

CORN MEAL PASTRY
125 g (4 oz) flour
a pinch of salt
60 g (2 oz) yellow corn meal
(or maize meal)
125 g (4 oz) chilled butter
45–60 ml (3–4 tbsp) cold water

Sift the flour and salt into a bowl. Stir in the corn meal (or maize meal). Cut in the butter and, using your fingertips, rub together lightly to form coarse crumbs. Gradually mix in enough cold water to form a soft dough; alternatively, use a food processor. Wrap well and chill until firm enough to handle.

SPICY CHICKEN FILLING
8 chicken portions
flour for dusting
30 ml (2 tbsp) oil
1 medium onion, finely chopped
2 red peppers, finely chopped
1 clove garlic, crushed
5 ml (1 tsp) chilli powder
(see page 9)
5 ml (1 tsp) ground cumin
5 ml (1 tsp) ground coriander
2 ripe tomatoes, skinned and
chopped
125 ml (4 fl oz) chicken stock
225 g (8 oz) fresh corn kernels
175 g (6 oz) cooked black-eye beans
15 g (½ oz) fresh coriander leaves
salt and freshly ground black pepper

Trim the chicken pieces, rinse and pat dry using paper towels. Season and dust with flour. Heat the oil and brown the chicken pieces on both sides, adding more oil if necessary. Remove the chicken pieces using a slotted spoon, and add the onion and the peppers to the pan, adding more oil if necessary. Cook gently until softened. Stir in the garlic, spices, tomatoes and a small amount of seasoning and cook for 5 minutes. Return the chicken to the pan and pour in the stock. Cover and cook for 25–30 minutes or until tender, turning once. Mix in the corn, beans and fresh coriander. Season to taste. Turn into an oiled pie dish and allow to cool.

Roll out the corn meal (or maize meal) pastry between two sheets of greaseproof paper, lightly floured if necessary. Wet the rim of the pie dish. Peel off one sheet of paper and invert the pastry over the pie dish. Press firmly onto the wetted edge and peel off the remaining paper. Trim the edge and crimp, using a fork. Bake the pie at 180 °C (350 °F; gas 4) for an hour or until the crust is golden brown and the filling is cooked and bubbly.
SERVES 4–6

ROASTED SPICED BABY CHICKENS

Whole baby chickens are quite impressive at a small dinner party, but if there's a substantial starter and a rich dessert to finish, the chickens could easily be split to serve eight.

4 baby chickens, about 500 g
(18 oz) each
45 g (1½ oz) melted butter
5 ml (1 tsp) ground turmeric
5 ml (1 tsp) ground cinnamon
2 cloves garlic, crushed
15 ml (1 tbsp) clear honey
salt and freshly ground black pepper

GARNISH
fresh mint leaves

Wash chickens well and remove any visible fat. Dry thoroughly using paper towels and season inside and out. Tie them up neatly. Place in a roasting tin just large enough to take them comfortably. Mix together the butter, spices, garlic and honey. Use to brush all over the chickens. Roast at 200 °C (400 °F; gas 6) for about 45 minutes or until nicely browned and tender. Turn off the oven and allow to stand for 10–15 minutes. Spoon over the pan juices and garnish with fresh mint. Serve with Curried Rice (see below), Fresh Green Chutney (see page 47) and a mix of steamed baby vegetables.
SERVES 4

CURRIED RICE

30 ml (2 tbsp) oil
1 onion, finely chopped
5 ml (1 tsp) mild curry powder
(see page 71)
200 g (7 oz) long-grain rice
1 clove garlic, crushed
500 ml (17 fl oz) hot chicken stock
1 stick (about 4 cm/1½ in)
cinnamon
60 ml (4 tbsp) seedless raisins
60 ml (4 tbsp) toasted, slivered
almonds
5 ml (1 tsp) salt

Blanch the raisins briefly by dropping them into boiling water. Leave to stand for 1–2 minutes and drain.

Heat the oil and soften the onion gently until pale golden. Stir in the curry powder, rice and garlic, and keep stirring for a few minutes. Add the stock, cinnamon and salt, and bring to the boil. Reduce heat, cover tightly and simmer gently for about 15 minutes or until the liquid is absorbed and the rice is tender.

Stir in the plumped raisins and toasted almonds and serve with Roasted Spiced Baby Chickens.
SERVES 4

FRESH GREEN CHUTNEY

60 g (2 oz) fresh coriander
or mint leaves
6 spring onions, sliced
1 clove garlic, crushed
1 slice (about 1.5 cm/½ in) fresh root
ginger, peeled and crushed
2 fresh green chillies, chopped
45 ml (3 tbsp) white wine
vinegar
5 ml (1 tsp) sugar
5 ml (1 tsp) salt

Blend or process all the ingredients for this unusual fresh chutney thoroughly to make a delicious accompaniment to the Roasted Spiced Baby Chickens and Curried Rice (see page 46).

BARBECUED CURRIED CHICKEN BREASTS

This mild dish works well on the barbecue. Serve with the curry sauce, Nasi Lemak (see page 59), a vinegar-dressed tomato, onion and fresh coriander salad and a sweet chutney.

8 chicken breast portions, skinned
and filleted

MARINADE
1 medium onion, finely chopped
30 ml (2 tbsp) sunflower oil
1 clove garlic, crushed
15 ml (1 tbsp) mild curry powder
(see page 71)
500 ml (17 fl oz) thick plain yoghurt
5 ml (1 tsp) flour
salt and freshly ground black pepper

Rinse the chicken, pat dry using paper towels and make a few slashes in each portion. Arrange in a single layer in a suitable dish. Soften the onion in the heated oil until pale golden. Stir in the garlic and curry powder and cook gently for about 1–2 minutes. Allow to cool and stir in the yoghurt. Add seasoning to taste. Pour the marinade over the chicken and leave, covered, in the refrigerator overnight. Bring back to room temperature before barbecuing. Remove the chicken from the marinade. Whisk the marinade with the flour and bring to the boil. Keep warm while barbecuing the chicken over hot coals until golden brown and cooked, but still moist and springy. Serve with the sauce.
SERVES 4

SPICY CHICKEN PIE WITH CORN MEAL PASTRY (PAGE 46)

ROASTED SPICED BABY CHICKENS SERVED WITH CURRIED RICE (BOTH PAGE 46) AND BRAISED CORN (PAGE 45)

CHICKEN WITH CHILLI AND BALSAMIC VINEGAR

This is an easy stir-fry, modern in its mix of an oriental method of cooking with distinctly Italian ingredients. A simple salad of sliced tomatoes sprinkled with balsamic vinegar makes a good accompaniment.

Balsamic vinegar is a red wine vinegar, boiled down to a sugar-rich syrup and aged in wood for many years. It has a deeper flavour than ordinary wine vinegar, being simultaneously sweet and spicy. The best balsamic vinegar comes from Modena in Italy. Understandably, it is very expensive. Luckily there are less expensive commercial types available which are also delicious.

500 g (18 oz) chicken breast portions, skinned and filleted
30 ml (2 tbsp) balsamic vinegar

MARINADE
30 ml (2 tbsp) olive oil
2 cloves garlic, crushed
1 fresh, red chilli, chopped
30 ml (2 tbsp) shredded fresh basil leaves
1.25 ml (¼ tsp) salt

STIR-FRIED CHICKEN WITH ORANGE & CHILLI

Bright with red pepper and green peas, this Chinese stir-fry is an attractive dish that is easy to prepare and interesting to eat with the flavours of orange and chilli.

500 g (18 oz) chicken breast fillets, skinned
1 red pepper
100 g (3½ oz) mangetout
or sugar snap peas
30 ml (2 tbsp) sunflower oil

SAUCE
15 ml (1 tbsp) cornflour
60 ml (4 tbsp) soy sauce
125 ml (4 fl oz) chicken stock
grated rind of a bright orange
125 ml (4 fl oz) fresh orange juice
15 ml (1 tbsp) sugar
15 ml (1 tbsp) vinegar
15 ml (1 tbsp) sesame oil
1 clove garlic, crushed
1 fresh, red chilli, chopped

GARNISH
sliced spring onions
or fresh coriander leaves

Slice the chicken thinly. Remove the seeds and core from the pepper and cut into short, thin strips. Trim the peas. Heat the oil in a wide pan or wok and, over a high heat, stir-fry the chicken for a few minutes until just cooked through. Remove using a slotted spoon.

Add the strips of pepper and the peas to the pan, and stir-fry for 1–2 minutes. Mix the ingredients for the sauce well and add the sauce to the pan. Simmer for a few minutes, stirring constantly, until vegetables are tender-crisp. Return the chicken to the pan and, while stirring, allow to heat through.

Garnish lightly with spring onions or coriander leaves and serve over steamed rice.
SERVES 3–4

GARNISH
fresh basil leaves

Slice the chicken breasts crosswise into strips. Mix the ingredients for the marinade together well. Mix the chicken with the marinade and allow to stand at room temperature for 30 minutes or refrigerate overnight. Bring back to room temperature before frying. Turn the chicken together with the marinade into a hot, heavy pan and stir-fry over a high heat for a few minutes until just cooked through and still moist. Pour in the balsamic vinegar and stir for 1–2 minutes.

Serve immediately with pasta tossed in a basil pesto, or in a mixture of olive oil with crushed garlic and chopped chilli.
SERVES 3–4

TANDOORI-STYLE SPICED CHICKEN

Nothing can match the wonderful taste of proper tandoori chicken cooked in the traditional oven. But this adaptation is very good – both with regard to spicing and the careful cooking technique.

6 chicken breast portions, skinned and filleted

SPICED TANDOORI MARINADE
5 ml (1 tsp) paprika
1.25 ml (¼ tsp) cayenne pepper
5 ml (1 tsp) ground turmeric
5 ml (1 tsp) ground cumin
5 ml (1 tsp) ground coriander
5 ml (1 tsp) garam masala
(see page 65)
1.25 ml (¼ tsp) nutmeg
1.25 ml (¼ tsp) cinnamon
2 cardamom pods, cracked
juice of 2 lemons
1 medium onion, chopped
a chunk (about 2 cm/¾ in) of fresh root ginger, peeled and chopped
250 ml (8 fl oz) plain yoghurt
30 ml (2 tbsp) tomato paste
5 ml (1 tsp) salt

GARNISH
shredded lettuce
onion rings
lemon wedges

Slash the chicken pieces, then arrange in a single layer in a shallow dish. Blend the ingredients for the marinade together and pour the marinade over. Allow the chicken pieces to marinate overnight in the refrigerator or for 1–2 hours at room temperature. Arrange the chicken together with the marinade in a single layer in a baking tin just the right size and bake at 190 °C (375 °F; gas 5) for 20 minutes. Remove the chicken and place on a rack in the same baking tin. Bake, basting now and again, for another 20 minutes or until the chicken is just cooked, springy to the touch and still moist. Turn onto a platter and garnish with shredded lettuce, onion rings and lemon wedges. Serve with steamed basmati rice.
SERVES 4–6

PORTUGUESE PIRI-PIRI CHICKEN

This is a quick dish to fit into a busy weekday schedule. Often I simply bake some potatoes, unpeeled and halved, along with the chicken. Sweet potatoes too are delicious, contrasting with the spiciness of the chicken.

1 chicken, spatchcocked
salt and freshly ground black pepper

PIRI-PIRI MARINADE
4–6 dried red chillies, sliced
60 ml (4 tbsp) lemon juice
60 ml (4 tbsp) olive oil
60 ml (4 tbsp) sunflower oil
3 cloves garlic, crushed

GARNISH
fresh coriander leaves

Cut the chicken down the backbone and open it out as flat as possible, pressing down on the breastbone. Rinse and pat dry using paper towels. Season and arrange skin side up in an oiled baking pan. Mix the ingredients for the marinade well. Pour the marinade over and leave in the refrigerator overnight or at room temperature for 1–2 hours. Roast at 190 °C (375 °F; gas 5) for an hour or until golden and tender. Serve with Spanish Rice (see right) and a salad.
SERVES 2–4

SPANISH RICE

30 ml (2 tbsp) olive oil
1 medium onion, chopped
1 green pepper, chopped
400 g (14 oz) long-grain rice
1 clove garlic, crushed
1 can (about 400 g/14 oz) tomatoes
500 ml (17 fl oz) hot chicken stock
30 ml (2 tbsp) sliced pimento-stuffed olives
30 ml (2 tbsp) chopped parsley
salt and freshly ground black pepper

Heat the oil and soften the onion and green pepper. Add the rice and stir for 1–2 minutes. Now stir in the garlic. Crush the tomatoes and add, together with the juice, the hot chicken stock and 5 ml (1 tsp) salt. Cover tightly and simmer for about 25 minutes or until the rice is tender and the liquid has been absorbed. Stir in olives and parsley and allow to stand, covered, for 5 minutes. Season to taste and serve.
SERVES 6

CURRIED ROAST CHICKEN WITH APPLES & CINNAMON

The simplest of ingredients combine to make the tastiest of dishes. Serve with roast potatoes, and chunks of parsnip roasted along with the potatoes.

1 chicken, about 1.5 kg (3 lb)
2 apples, peeled and cut into slim wedges
1 small onion, thinly sliced
2–3 sticks (about 4 cm/1½ in each) cinnamon
15 ml (1 tbsp) curry powder
15 ml (1 tbsp) sunflower oil
salt and freshly ground black pepper

SAUCE
250 ml (8 fl oz) chicken stock
60 ml (4 tbsp) single (thin) cream

GRILLED CHICKEN WITH CHILLI AND RED PEPPER (THIS PAGE), STIR-FRIED CHICKEN WITH ORANGE AND CHILLI (PAGE 49)

Wash the chicken well and remove any visible fat. Dry thoroughly using paper towels and season inside and out. Stuff the chicken with the apples mixed with the onion, and tuck in a few cinnamon sticks. Mix the curry powder with the oil and spoon it all over the chicken. Place the chicken on its one side in a roasting tin of a suitable size and roast at 200 °C (400 °F; gas 6) for about 20 minutes. Turn the chicken onto the other side and roast again for 20 minutes. Now place the chicken breast side up and roast for a further 20 minutes or until it is golden brown, crisp and tender. Remove to a heated platter. To make the sauce, pour the stock into the roasting tin and cook over a high heat, stirring all the time to loosen any browned bits. Add the cream and reduce slightly over a high heat. Season to taste.

SERVES 4

GRILLED CHICKEN WITH CHILLI & RED PEPPER

Try this example of so-called Cal-Mex cookery, the most up-to-date adaptation of Mexican cooking. The accompaniments are typically Mexican – chilli, peppers, sweetcorn and avocado – but the treatment is light and contemporary.

500 g chicken breast portions, skinned and filleted
I large red pepper

MARINADE
75 ml (2½ fl oz) olive oil
juice of a lemon or lime
I fresh chilli, chopped
I small onion, peeled and finely chopped
I clove garlic, crushed
5 ml (I tsp) ground coriander
salt and freshly ground black pepper

GARNISH
fresh coriander leaves
lemon or lime wedges

Rinse the chicken portions and pat dry using paper towels. Slice the red pepper into broad strips. Mix all the ingredients for the marinade together thoroughly. Marinate the chicken and pepper strips for an hour at room temperature.

Slide the chicken under a pre-heated grill for 4–5 minutes on each side or until it is lightly browned and firm, but still quite moist and springy to the touch. Alternatively, pan-grill or barbecue. At the same time, grill the peppers until softened.

Serve the chicken and red pepper strips with sliced avocado, buttered baby corn and warm tortillas. Garnish with fresh green coriander leaves and lemon or lime wedges.

SERVES 4

Meat

This is real food – gutsy, hearty main courses
that take star place on any menu, needing little else for
starters or afters. If eating less meat suits your lifestyle, bear it
in mind for a winter dinner party or a summer barbecue. And it's
great to share a bowl of spicy chilli with friends for a casual supper.

FROM A DINNER FOR SIX: *STIR-FRIED LAMB AND CHILLI SERVED WITH SPINACH RICE* (BOTH PAGE 61)

MOROCCAN COUSCOUS

Follow the instructions carefully, and you'll soon grasp how easy it is to prepare this dish. It's great – wonderful for a dinner party. Do as the Moroccans do, and follow with a chilled orange salad for dessert, dotted with chopped dates, fragrant with rose water (obtainable from Indian grocers) and delicately spiced with cinnamon.

150 g (5 oz) butter
1 kg (2¼ lb) lean leg or shoulder
of lamb, cut into 8 large chunks
8 chicken portions
500 g (18 oz) onions, quartered
2.5 ml (½ tsp) saffron
or 5 ml (1 tsp) ground turmeric
3–4 sticks (about 4 cm/1½ in each)
cinnamon
a handful of fresh coriander leaves
5 ml (1 tsp) harissa paste
(see page 8)
750 g (1¾ lb) ripe, red tomatoes,
skinned, seeds removed, quartered
1.25–1.5 litres (2¼–2¾ pints) water
500 g (18 oz) carrots, scraped
and thickly sliced
500 g (18 oz) turnips, peeled
and cut into chunks
500 g (18 oz) courgettes,
thickly sliced
2 red peppers, seeds removed, sliced
1 can (about 400 g/14 oz) chickpeas
45 g (1½ oz) seedless raisins
500 g (18 oz) large chunks of
peeled pumpkin
salt and freshly ground black pepper

500 g (18 oz) couscous
(see note)
750 ml (1¼ pints) boiling water
(optional)
harissa paste (see page 8)

GARNISH
fresh coriander leaves

NOTE: Couscous is usually available
in packets from most delicatessens
and major supermarkets.

Melt 100 g (3½ oz) of the butter in a large, heavy casserole dish and stir in the lamb, chicken and onions. Cook over fairly high heat, stirring often, until the mixture browns nicely. Add saffron or turmeric, the cinnamon, coriander, the 5 ml (1 tsp) harissa paste and a little seasoning. Stir in the tomatoes and water, and bring to the boil. Remove any scum. Reduce the heat and simmer for an hour. Add the carrots and turnips and simmer for another 30 minutes. Add the courgettes, red peppers, chickpeas and raisins and cook for about 20 minutes or until tender. Season to taste. In a separate saucepan, steam the pumpkin pieces until tender but still intact.

To prepare the couscous, pour 750 ml (1¼ pints) boiling water or the hot cooking liquid over the couscous and stir in the remaining butter and some salt. Leave for 5–10 minutes until the liquid has been absorbed. Fluff up with a fork and place in a shallow, buttered baking dish. If you like, dot with more butter. Cover tightly and then bake at 180 °C (350 °F; gas 4) for 20 minutes, stirring once half-way.

To serve, place the hot couscous on a large heated platter. If you like, toss with a little butter. Moisten with some of the cooking liquid and pile the meat and the vegetables in the centre. Surround with the pumpkin. Garnish with fresh coriander leaves. Serve with the cooking liquid as a sauce. Pass round the harissa paste, which can be diluted with the cooking liquid to suit your taste.
SERVES 8

TEX-MEX CHILLI

Texans love Mexican food. However, over the years they've changed and adapted it, resulting in a Tex-Mex cuisine that's as well known as the original. This dish is addictive!

60 ml (4 tbsp) sunflower oil
2 medium onions, chopped
1 kg (2¼ lb) stewing beef, diced
250 g (9 oz) lean minced beef
2 cloves garlic, crushed
60 ml (4 tbsp) Mexican spice mix
(see note)
1 can (about 400 g/14 oz) tomatoes,
crushed
5 ml (1 tsp) sugar
1 bay leaf
1 can (about 400 g/14 oz) red kidney
beans, drained
salt and freshly ground black pepper

thick, soured cream
grated mild Cheddar cheese
red chilli sauce

NOTE: A ready-made Mexican spice mix is usually available from most supermarkets.

Heat half the oil in a heavy casserole dish. Add the onions and cook gently until softened, but still pale. Now add the remaining oil, stir in the meat and cook over a high heat until the meat changes colour. Stir in the garlic and Mexican spice mix and cook for a minute. Add the crushed tomatoes, sugar, bay leaf and some seasoning. Bring to a simmer, then cover tightly and bake at 160 °C (325 °F; gas 3) for 1¼ hours or until very tender. Add the drained beans and cook further until thoroughly heated through. Season to taste.

Serve generously in bowls topped with grated cheese and thick, soured cream. Pass round a strong red chilli sauce at table for the really hardened chilli-lovers.
SERVES 6

CHILLI & BEANS FOR A CROWD

This is a real party dish, impressively easy, affordable and sublime to eat. Have lots of chilled beer or bottles of a red house wine. Chunks of fresh fruit – iced melons in summer – are all you'll need for dessert.

60 ml (4 tbsp) oil
3 large onions, chopped
2 large green peppers, cored, seeds removed, finely chopped
4 cloves garlic, crushed
2 kg (4½ lb) lean, minced beef
500 g (18 oz) spicy sausage
15 ml (1 tbsp) dried oregano
30 g (1 oz) chopped parsley
30 ml (2 tbsp) ground cumin
60 ml (4 tbsp) chilli powder (see page 9)
1 can (about 400 g/14 oz) tomato purée
1 can (about 125 g/4 oz) tomato paste
4 cans (about 400 g/14 oz each) tomatoes, crushed
2 cans (about 400 g/14 oz each) red kidney beans, drained
salt and freshly ground black pepper

thick, soured cream
grated mild Cheddar cheese

Heat the oil in a large, heavy casserole. Add the onions and peppers, cover and cook gently, stirring occasionally, until softened. Stir in the garlic. Add the mince and cook over a brisk heat, stirring often, until it changes colour. Remove the skin or casing from the sausage, crumble and stir into the mince. Add the herbs and spices. Mix in the tomato purée, paste and crushed tomatoes. Add some seasoning. Stir well and bring to a simmer. Reduce the heat, cover and cook gently for 1½ hours or until very tender. Add the drained beans and heat through. Check the seasoning and adjust if necessary. Serve in deep bowls. Top with thick, soured cream and a generous grating of mild Cheddar. Serve with Tomato and Corn Salsa (see below) and a salad of shredded lettuce, chopped avocado, fresh coriander leaves and onion, tossed in a lemon and oil dressing.
SERVES 16–20

TOMATO & CORN SALSA

4 medium corn-on-the-cob
4 large, firm, red tomatoes, chopped
2 fresh green chillies, chopped
60 ml (4 tbsp) chopped fresh coriander leaves
juice of 1 lemon
salt and freshly ground black pepper

Slice the corn off the cob. Blanch for barely a minute in a saucepan of boiling water. Drain and rinse under cold running water. Mix with the rest of the ingredients, seasoning to taste. If it's not hot enough, add more chopped chillies or a dash or two of Tabasco sauce.

ENTRECÔTE STEAKS WITH SPICY AVOCADO SAUCE

Superbly grilled steaks go well with this fine sauce. Share them with your best friends, as they are a real treat.

4 medium entrecôte steaks (about 150 g/5 oz each)
olive oil for brushing

SAUCE
1 large ripe avocado, skinned and chopped
1 ripe, red tomato, skinned, seeds removed
45 ml (3 tbsp) olive oil
15 ml (1 tbsp) red wine vinegar
2–3 fresh green chillies, seeds removed, chopped
1 extra large hard-boiled egg, chopped
30 ml (2 tbsp) chopped fresh coriander
salt and freshly ground black pepper

To make the sauce, mix all the ingredients together carefully in a processor or blender to make a chunky sauce. Season to taste.

Pat the steaks dry using paper towels, then brush with oil and grill until nicely browned, but still moist and rare inside. Spoon the sauce generously on top of the steaks and serve with sautéed potatoes.
SERVES 4

CHILLI BEEF PIE WITH FILO (THIS PAGE)

CHILLI BEEF PIE WITH FILO

A Tex-Mex filling is topped with Greek pastry. The crumpled sheets of filo (also called 'phyllo') make the prettiest topping, and, as they say, it's as easy as pie. Serve simply, with a salad of shredded lettuce, avocado, tomato and onion.

60 ml (4 tbsp) oil
1 kg (2¼ lb) lean stewing beef,
cut into chunks of about 2 x 2 cm
(¾ x ¾ in)
2 medium onions, chopped
2 cloves garlic, crushed
2 cans (about 400 g/14 oz each)
tomatoes
1 small can (about 125 g/4 oz)
tomato paste
500 ml (17 fl oz) beef stock
30–45 ml (2–3 tbsp) chilli powder
(see page 9)
15 ml (1 tbsp) ground cumin
15 ml (1 tbsp) dried oregano
15 ml (1 tbsp) cornflour
1 can (about 400 g/14 oz)
pinto beans
250 g (9 oz) spicy sausage, grilled
and cut into chunks of about
1 x 1 cm (¼ x ¼ in)
8 sheets filo pastry
melted butter or oil
salt and freshly ground black pepper

In a heavy casserole dish, heat the oil and brown the beef in batches over a high heat. Once nicely browned, remove using a slotted spoon and set aside. Add the onion to the casserole, add more oil if necessary and cook gently until softened. Stir in the garlic, then return the browned beef to the casserole along with the chopped tomatoes, the juice from the can, tomato paste, stock, chilli powder, cumin, oregano, salt and pepper. Cover and simmer for about 1½ hours or until the meat is quite tender. Using a slotted spoon, transfer the mixture to a greased pie dish. Mix the cornflour to a smooth paste with a little cold water. Use it to thicken 250 ml (8 fl oz) of the cooking liquid. Allow to cool and mix in the beans and sausage. Turn into the pie dish and mix with the meat. Brush two sheets of the filo with melted butter or oil. Place over the pie dish, pressing it down firmly around the sides. Now brush the remaining sheets of pastry with melted butter or oil and crumple each sheet with your hands. Arrange the crumpled sheets of pastry on top of the pie and bake at 220 °C (425 °F; gas 7) for 20–30 minutes until crisp and golden and piping hot.

SERVES 6

SATAY

These delicious skewers of barbecued meats are popular all over Thailand, Malaysia, Singapore and Indonesia. In these hot climates, they would be grilled outdoors as street food, or at informal cafés. There would be variations in the make-up of the marinade, and in Muslim areas of Malaysia pork would, of course, not be included.

250 g (9 oz) pork fillet
250 g (9 oz) beef fillet
250 g (9 oz) skinned and filleted chicken breast

MARINADE
2.5 ml (½ tsp) turmeric
1.25 ml (¼ tsp) salt
250 ml (8 fl oz) thick coconut milk (see page 11)
spicy peanut sauce (see right)

Cut the meats and chicken with the grain into strips about 10 cm (4 in) long and 1 cm (½ in) wide. Soften the skewers by soaking in warm water for about an hour. Mix the ingredients for the marinade well. Place the strips of meat and chicken in the marinade for about an hour at room temperature or overnight in the refrigerator. Thread lengthwise, using one skewer for each satay, in a zigzag fashion to ensure that the meat is held firmly. Grill for a few minutes on a well-oiled rack over coals or under a preheated grill, turning once. Serve with a Spicy Peanut Sauce (see right) and a Thai Cucumber Salad (see page 66).
SERVES 4–6

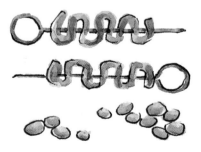

SPICY PEANUT SAUCE

3 fresh or dried red chillies
2 large cloves garlic
30 ml (2 tbsp) lemon grass, stalk ends crushed, then thinly sliced
15 ml (1 tbsp) finely chopped spring onion
6 coriander roots plus the stems, finely chopped
2.5 ml (½ tsp) grated rind of a lime or lemon
6 peppercorns
2.5 ml (½ tsp) shrimp paste (see page 11)
(or a pounded, salted anchovy fillet)
250 ml (8 fl oz) coconut milk
15 ml (1 tbsp) Thai fish sauce (see page 11)
30 ml (2 tbsp) sugar
15 ml (1 tbsp) tamarind juice (see page 11)
60 ml (4 tbsp) crushed, roasted peanuts

If you are using dried chillies, soak them first for about 15 minutes, then drain. Remove the seeds and membrane for a milder flavour, then chop the chillies finely. Using a pestle and mortar pound the chillies, garlic, lemon grass, spring onion, coriander and the rind individually, then mix together. Crush the peppercorns separately and pound with the shrimp paste. Add this to the first lot of pounded ingredients, mixing together well. Over a high heat, reduce 125 ml (4 fl oz) coconut milk by half. Add the pounded ingredients and stir-fry for barely a minute, until just fragrant. Add the fish sauce, sugar and tamarind juice. Stir-fry until the sugar has dissolved. Add the crushed peanuts, then gradually add the remaining coconut milk, stirring until well blended. If the sauce needs more blending, remove from the hob and run a hand-held electric blender through it. Return it to the hob and simmer until reduced and thickened. Serve the peanut sauce at room temperature.

SPICED TROPICAL LAMB

A deliciously different curried dish that uses fresh fruit and vegetables and wine. The use of rum gives away its West Indian origins.

45 ml (3 tbsp) oil
1.5 kg (3½ lb) boned shoulder of lamb, cubed
2 medium onions, finely chopped
2 cloves garlic, crushed
30 ml (2 tbsp) curry powder
250 ml (8 fl oz) orange juice
grated rind of an orange
600 ml (1 pint) dry white wine
2 whole cloves
2 cardamom pods, cracked
1 stick (about 4 cm/1½ in) cinnamon
1 not-too-ripe mango or small pawpaw, peeled and chopped
500 g (18 oz) baby new potatoes, halved
500 g (18 oz) butternut, squash or pumpkin, peeled and cubed
250 g (9 oz) courgettes, thickly sliced
30 ml (2 tbsp) rum
salt and pepper

In a heavy saucepan, heat 15 ml (1 tbsp) of the oil. Add the lamb in batches and sauté for approximately 5 minutes on each side or until well browned, adding more oil if needed. Remove using a slotted spoon and season lightly. Add the remaining oil to the saucepan, reduce the heat and stir in the onion. Cook very gently until pale golden and softened. Add a little salt and, if necessary, a little water to prevent the onion catching. Stir in the garlic and curry powder, then pour in the orange juice and rind. Cook for a few minutes, then stir in the wine and bring to the boil. Reduce heat, add the browned meat, spices, fruit and vegetables and season lightly. Cover and simmer for 45 minutes or until the lamb is very tender. Lastly, stir in the rum.

Season to taste and serve with Roti breads (see page 63) or steamed rice and chutney.
SERVES 6

Nasi Goreng (this page), Satay with Spicy Peanut Sauce (page 56)

NASI GORENG

*This Indonesian dish is
a marvellous combination of tastes
and textures. The Dutch colonists
took the recipe home with them and
today it's probably as popular in
Holland as in the East Indies.*

75 ml (2½ fl oz) oil for frying
2 extra large eggs
1 medium onion, thinly sliced
2 medium onions, finely chopped
2 cloves garlic, crushed
5 ml (1 tsp) sambal oelek
(Indonesian chilli paste)
(see note)
5 ml (1 tsp) sambal trassie oedang
(Indonesian shrimp paste)
(see note)
200 g (7 oz) uncooked shrimps or
small prawns, shelled and deveined
250 g (9 oz) diced, cooked chicken
or veal
200 g (7 oz) cooked long-grain rice
30 ml (2 tbsp) soy sauce
5 ml (1 tsp) sugar
15 ml (1 tbsp) lemon juice
125 g (4 oz) cooked ham,
cut into strips
salt and freshly ground black pepper

soy sauce
chilli paste (see pages 8–9)

NOTE: These pastes, imported from Indonesia, are available from major supermarkets or from speciality oriental shops.

Heat 15 ml (1 tbsp) of the oil in a pan and pour in the beaten eggs to make a thin omelette. Cut the omelette into very thin strips and keep warm. Add 30 ml (2 tbsp) oil and fry the sliced onion until brown and crisp and set aside.

Wipe out the pan and add 30 ml (2 tbsp) oil. Add the chopped onion, garlic and the pastes. Cook gently until softened. Add the shrimps. Stir-fry for 5 minutes or until cooked through. Stir in the diced chicken or veal. Then add the rice, soy sauce, sugar, lemon juice and some seasoning. Stir-fry until the rice is hot and lightly browned.

Season to taste and serve topped with omelette and ham strips and the fried onion. Pass round soy sauce and chilli paste.

This dish is particularly good when served with fried, battered banana pieces and crispy, puffed prawn crackers.
SERVES 3–4

CHILLI BEEF PIE WITH CORN CUSTARD TOPPING

This is one of my favourite dishes. It comes from South America, but it is much like a spicy version of the South African bobotie (see page 68).

BEEF FILLING
45 ml (3 tbsp) oil
2 medium onions, finely chopped
I red or green pepper, seeds removed, chopped
750 g (1¾ lb) lean minced beef
2 cloves garlic, crushed
5 ml (1 tsp) chilli powder
5 ml (1 tsp) ground cumin
5 ml (1 tsp) ground coriander
I stick (about 4 cm/1½ in) cinnamon
5 ml (1 tsp) dried oregano
30 ml (2 tbsp) red wine vinegar
2.5 ml (½ tsp) sugar
I can (about 400 g/14 oz) tomatoes, crushed
60 ml (4 tbsp) seedless raisins
30 ml (2 tbsp) chopped parsley
30 ml (2 tbsp) chopped fresh coriander leaves
salt and freshly ground black pepper

CORN CUSTARD
450 g (1 lb) fresh corn kernels, blanched
4 extra large eggs
125 ml (4 fl oz) soured cream
5 ml (1 tsp) salt

To make the beef filling, heat the oil in a large, heavy pan and add the onion and peppers. Cook gently until softened. Add the mince and keep stirring until the meat changes colour. Stir in the garlic, spices, oregano, vinegar, sugar, crushed tomatoes plus the juice from the can and some seasoning. Bring to a simmer, then cover tightly and simmer for about 10–15 minutes. Blanch the raisins briefly by pouring boiling water over them, then strain. Now stir the raisins, parsley and fresh coriander leaves into the mince mixture. Season to taste and turn into an oiled baking dish.

To make the corn custard, blend the corn, eggs, cream and salt in a processor or blender so that it still has a rough texture. Pour the mixture over the beef filling and bake at 190 °C (375 °F; gas 5) for about 40 minutes or until golden and set. Allow to stand for 10 minutes before cutting it into squares.

Serve with steamed brown rice and a tomato, avocado and crisp lettuce salad.
SERVES 6–8

BARBECUED STEAKS WITH SPICY BASIL PESTO

A starry summer night is the time to invest in the best of steaks to barbecue immaculately and serve with this most delicious of sauces. Grill vegetables on the barbecue to serve with the steaks: wedges of bright sweet peppers, split courgettes and spring onions, slices of aubergine, each first moistened with olive oil.

6 thick sirloin steaks (about 200 g/7 oz each)
olive oil for brushing
coarse sea salt

PESTO
125 g (4 oz) fresh basil leaves, chopped
3 cloves garlic, crushed
3 fresh green chillies, finely chopped
60 ml (4 tbsp) olive oil
salt

To make the pesto, pound the ingredients together in a food processor until the mixture reaches a fairly smooth consistency. Pat the steaks dry using paper towels, then brush with oil. Grill over hot coals for a few minutes on each side until browned, but still rare inside. Season with salt (milled) and top with the pesto. Serve with grilled vegetables and baked potatoes.
SERVES 6

BEEF RENDANG

A rendang is a Malaysian dish in which the meat (or chicken) is braised with spices and coconut milk until the sauce has been reduced so that the meat is almost dry.

500 g (18 oz) topside or rump steak
15–30 ml (1–2 tbsp) chilli paste (see pages 8–9)
8 shallots or fat spring onions
2 fat cloves garlic
2 stalks lemon grass, stalk ends crushed
I thick slice (about 2 cm/¾ inch) of fresh root ginger, peeled
500 ml (17 fl oz) coconut milk (see page 11)
5 ml (1 tsp) turmeric
2.5 ml (½ tsp) salt
15 ml (1 tbsp) tamarind juice (see page 11)

Ask your butcher to cut the meat into very thin slices (approximately 5 mm/¼ in wide). Cut across again into small squares. Slice the shallots, garlic and lemon grass. Peel and grate the ginger. Pour the coconut milk into a suitable saucepan. Add all the remaining ingredients except for the tamarind juice. Bring the mixture to the boil, then reduce the heat and simmer, uncovered, stirring from time to time to prevent sticking, until the meat is very tender and almost dry.

If necessary, remove the tender meat and allow the sauce to reduce. Lastly, stir in the tamarind juice and season to taste. Serve with Nasi Lemak (see page 59).
SERVES 4

CHILLI BEEF PIE WITH CORN CUSTARD TOPPING (PAGE 58)

NASI LEMAK

This Malaysian coconut rice is the basis of the traditional Malaysian breakfast that is now sold at hawkers' stalls throughout the day. The simplest version consists of the rice with some fried ikan bilis (dried anchovies), fresh cucumber slices and a chilli sambal.

COCONUT RICE
350 g (12 oz) Thai rice
(see note)
500 ml (17 fl oz) thin coconut milk
(see page 11)
1 screwpine leaf (optional)
(see page 11)
a grating of fresh root ginger
5 ml (1 tsp) salt
125 ml (4 fl oz) thick coconut milk
(see page 11)

GARNISH
roasted peanuts
sliced fresh cucumber
halved hard-boiled eggs
fried ikan bilis (dried anchovies)
sliced chillies or chilli sambal

NOTE: Thai rice is available from most supermarkets.

Soak the rice for at least an hour. Drain it and place in a suitable saucepan. Now pour over the thin coconut milk. Add the screwpine, if using, the ginger and salt. Cover and bring to a simmer. Cook for about 15 minutes or until the liquid is absorbed. Pour over the thick coconut milk. Turn off the heat, cover pan and leave on hob for about 10 minutes or until milk has been absorbed and rice is tender.

Serve the rice with Malaysian Chicken Curry (see page 65) or Beef Rendang (see page 58) as topping. Fried water spinach, which is found in Malaysia, is a traditional accompaniment. Or substitute stir-fried baby spinach leaves, hotted up with chilli.
SERVES 6

SPICY LAMB STEW WITH ROAST SWEET POTATOES (THIS PAGE); MANGO AND BEEF STIR-FRY (PAGE 61)

SPICY LAMB STEW WITH ROAST SWEET POTATOES

If you want to impress at a dinner party, you could not do better than choose this dish. The mix of spices adds up to a superb flavour, and the delicate sweetness of the sweet potatoes is splendid with the spiciness of the lamb.

75 ml (2½ fl oz) sunflower oil
2 kg (4½ lb) boned leg of lamb, cubed
(but ask the butcher for
the lamb bones)
2–3 large onions, chopped
3 cloves garlic, crushed
a chunk (about 2 cm/¾ in) of fresh
root ginger, peeled and crushed
45 ml (3 tbsp) ground cumin
30 ml (2 tbsp) ground coriander
30 ml (2 tbsp) flour
500 ml (17 fl oz) chicken stock

45 ml (3 tbsp) fresh lime
or lemon juice
2–3 fresh green chillies, chopped
1 can (about 400 g/14 oz) tomatoes,
crushed
salt and freshly ground black pepper

4–6 medium sweet potatoes
oil for moistening

GARNISH
fresh coriander leaves

Heat the oil in a large, heavy saucepan. Add the cubed lamb in batches and sauté until nicely browned, then remove using a slotted spoon and season lightly. Do the same with the bones, as they intensify the flavour of the dish.

Add the onions, garlic, ginger and spices and cook gently until the onions are softened. Season lightly. Stir in the flour and keep stirring for 1–2 minutes. Stir in the chicken stock, lime or lemon juice, chillies and tomatoes together with the juice. Bring to a simmer, stirring all the time. Return the lamb and bones to the saucepan, cover and simmer gently for about 1½ hours or until the lamb is very tender. Season to taste and discard the lamb bones.

Remove the lamb to a warm platter using a slotted spoon and keep warm while reducing the sauce to a good consistency over a high heat. Season to taste. Pour over the lamb and garnish with coriander leaves.

To roast the sweet potatoes, first scrub and dry them. Halve lengthwise and moisten lightly with oil. Roast at 220 °C (425 °F; gas 7) for 45–60 minutes or until very tender. Season lightly to taste.
SERVES 8

STIR-FRIED LAMB & CHILLI

This sophisticated dish, inspired by the tastes of the Orient, uses the contemporary eclectic style of merging East and West. The mix of flavours makes this dish the star of a smart dinner party menu.

60 ml (4 tbsp) sunflower oil
750 g (1¾ lb) boned leg of lamb, cut into thin strips
(about 1 cm/½ in wide)
250 g (9 oz) onions, thinly sliced into half-moons
2 red peppers, seeds removed, thinly sliced
3 fresh red chillies, sliced
2 cloves garlic, crushed
a chunk (about 2 cm/¾ in) of fresh root ginger, peeled and crushed
6 cardamom pods, cracked
30 ml (2 tbsp) cumin seeds
5 ml (1 tsp) cornflour
125 ml (4 fl oz) beef stock
15 ml (1 tbsp) soy sauce
15 ml (1 tbsp) dry sherry
salt

Heat half the oil in a wide, heavy saucepan. Add the lamb and stir-fry over a high heat until browned. Remove using a slotted spoon and set aside. Season lightly. Add the remaining oil and the onions, peppers, chillies, garlic, ginger and spices to the pan, and stir-fry for 5 minutes until the vegetables are starting to soften. Return the lamb to the pan. Slake the cornflour with the stock, soy and sherry and pour into the pan. Allow to heat through and thicken slightly. Season to taste. Serve with Spinach Rice (see right).
SERVES 4–6

MANGO & BEEF STIR-FRY

The mangoes add an exotic, tropical flavour, their juicy sweetness contrasting exquisitely with the chilli and ginger.

400 g (14 oz) tender beef steak, cut into strips (about 1 cm/½ in wide)
15 ml (1 tbsp) sunflower oil
15 ml (1 tbsp) soy sauce
5 ml (1 tsp) dry sherry
2 not-too-ripe stringless mangoes or baby pawpaws, cut into strips
(about 1 cm/½ in wide)
salt and freshly ground black pepper

MARINADE
15 ml (1 tbsp) soy sauce
10 ml (2 tsp) dry sherry
10 ml (2 tsp) cornflour
1 fresh red chilli, chopped
a chunk (about 2 cm/¾ in) of fresh root ginger, peeled and crushed

GARNISH
fresh coriander leaves

Mix the ingredients for the marinade well. Now mix the beef with the marinade and allow to stand for 10 minutes. Heat the oil in a wok or large, heavy frying pan. Add the beef and stir-fry over a high heat for a few minutes until browned. Stir in the soy sauce and 5 ml (1 tsp) of sherry, add the mango strips and stir-fry until heated through. Season to taste. Sprinkle with coriander and serve immediately with Coconut Rice (see right) or with Thai rice, (available from most supermarkets).
SERVES 2–4

COCONUT RICE

200 g (7 oz) long-grain rice
60 ml (4 tbsp) desiccated coconut
1 stick (about 4 cm/1½ in) cinnamon
2 cardamom pods, cracked
15 g (½ oz) butter
500 ml (17 fl oz) water
squeeze of lemon juice
5 ml (1 tsp) salt

Place ingredients in a saucepan. Bring to the boil, then reduce heat and cover. Cook for 20 minutes or until all the liquid has evaporated and the rice is tender. Fluff up with a fork and serve with Mango and Beef Stir-Fry (see left) or with Spiced Tropical Lamb (see page 56).
SERVES 4–6

SPINACH RICE

200 g (7 oz) basmati rice
5 ml (1 tsp) salt
175 g (6 oz) washed spinach leaves, finely shredded
30 g (1 oz) butter

To prepare the rice, cook with the salt according to the manufacturer's instructions. When tender, drain and steam with the shreds of spinach for about 5 minutes. Stir in the butter and season to taste.
  Serve with Stir-Fried Lamb and Chilli (see left).
SERVES 4–6

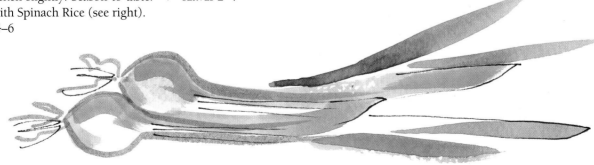

Curries

A substantial curry, with interesting sambals
(traditional accompaniments) and chutneys, makes a meal
of a dish, ideal for easy entertaining. While some with sensitive
palates may prefer a gently spiced and aromatic curry, those
with bolder tastes will go for a strong, rather robust recipe. Others
may relish the dishes that are slightly sweet with a fruity tang.

CURRYING FRIENDS WITH DHAL (PAGE 67), ROTI (PAGE 63), POPPADOMS, CHICKEN CURRY (PAGE 66) AND FRIED AUBERGINES (PAGE 67)

SPICED FISH

Indian in origin, this dish is aromatic, yet delicate in flavour. A little fish goes a long way, accompanied by a substantial roti bread. The making of a really good roti requires some expertise, so it may be more convenient to buy some from an Indian take-away. Otherwise, try the recipe on the right.

sunflower oil for frying
250 g (9 oz) firm white fish fillets

CURRY PASTE
2.5 ml (½ tsp) cumin seeds
2.5 ml (½ tsp) coriander seeds
3 cardamom pods, cracked
2.5 ml (½ tsp) ground turmeric
2.5 ml (½ tsp) peppercorns
1.25 ml (¼ tsp) chilli powder
(see page 9)
30 ml (2 tbsp) water

SAUCE
1 small onion, chopped
2 cloves garlic, chopped
2.5 ml (½ tsp) ground ginger
2.5 ml (½ tsp) ground cinnamon
30 ml (2 tbsp) ground almonds
1 bay leaf
2 ripe, red tomatoes, grated
125 ml (4 fl oz) fish stock or water
30 ml (2 tbsp) lemon juice
salt and freshly ground black pepper

GARNISH
4 spring onions, thinly sliced
fresh coriander leaves

First make the curry paste. Pound together the spices using a small food processor and mix with the water to form a paste. Set aside.

Bring 30 ml (2 tbsp) of oil to a moderate heat and brown the fish; then reduce the heat and allow fish to cook through for 5–10 minutes until it flakes easily. Remove the fish, and when cool, flake. To the same pan, add the onion, garlic, ginger, cinnamon, ground almonds and bay leaf and cook gently for 5–10 minutes or until golden. Add a little more oil if necessary. Stir in the prepared curry paste and cook gently for 3–4 minutes. Add the tomatoes and stock, or water, and leave to simmer until reduced and thickened. Add the flaked fish and allow to heat through. Stir in the lemon juice and seasoning to taste.

Garnish with the spring onions and coriander leaves. Serve with warm roti breads (see below) and a cucumber sambal (see right).
SERVES 2–4

ROTI

500 g (18 oz) flour
10 ml (2 tsp) salt
375 ml (12 fl oz) water
125 g (4 oz) butter
oil for frying

Mix the flour, salt and enough water (about 375 ml/12 fl oz) to make a soft dough. Knead lightly. Roll out, dot with butter and fold up as for puff pastry. Roll out again. Continue buttering, folding and rolling out, until all the butter has been used up. Set aside for at least 3 hours.

Next, roll out the dough into 6 thinnish rounds. Heat an iron pan or griddle. Brush thinly with oil. Place one round of dough in the pan and brush the top with oil. Cook until well browned underneath. Turn and brown on the other side. When browned, remove the roti from the pan and fold in half and then in quarters between two pieces of brown paper. Clap quickly between the hands in order to loosen the layers formed by the buttering-rolling procedure. Unfold and keep warm until serving.
MAKES 6

CUCUMBER SAMBAL

225 g (8 oz) grated cucumber
250 ml (8 fl oz) plain yoghurt

Strain the yoghurt for approximately 30 minutes to get rid of most of the whey. Salt the grated cucumber lightly and drain. Then simply mix the cucumber and yoghurt together.
SERVES 2–4

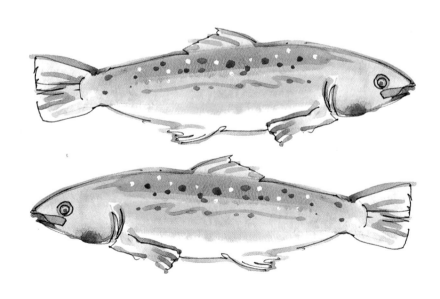

CURRIED HAKE (PAGE 65) WITH A LIME PICKLE ACCOMPANIMENT

CREAMY CURRIED SOLE WITH PINEAPPLE & MINT

Typical of a Caribbean style of curry, this dish is gentle and creamy. It's perfect with the subtlety of sole, but you can substitute a more economical fish, as long as it's a white, mild variety.

45 g (1½ oz) butter
2 medium onions, finely chopped
1 clove garlic, crushed
10 ml (2 tsp) peeled, chopped,
fresh root ginger
15 ml (1 tbsp) flour
15 ml (1 tbsp) mild curry powder
(see page 71)
250 ml (8 fl oz) single (thin) cream
500 g (18 oz) sole, skinned
and filleted
1 small pineapple, peeled
and cut into strips
strained fish stock (optional)
salt and freshly ground black pepper

GARNISH
60 ml (4 tbsp) toasted coconut
(see note)
60 ml (4 tbsp) toasted almonds
fresh mint

NOTE: Toast the desiccated coconut in a heated, dry frying pan, stirring all the time.

Melt half the butter. Add the onion, garlic and ginger and cook very gently for 20 minutes until softened and golden. Now mix the flour and curry powder together and stir into the onion mixture. Cook for 1–2 minutes, stirring all the time. Gradually pour in the cream and cook, still stirring, until thickened.

Cut the sole into narrow strips and stir-fry in the remaining hot butter until opaque. Add to the curry sauce with the pineapple strips and heat through. If the sauce seems too thick, thin it down with a little strained fish stock. Season to taste, then sprinkle with the

coconut and almonds and scatter the chopped fresh mint on top to garnish. Serve this dish with steamed rice and chutney.
SERVES 3–4

CURRIED HAKE

Hake, fresh or frozen, adapts well to a spicy treatment. This recipe, with its readily available ingredients, is one that you will use often, particularly for family meals.

1 kg (2¼ lb) hake, skinned and filleted
60 g (2 oz) butter
15 ml (1 tbsp) sunflower oil
3 medium onions, thinly sliced
a chunk (about 2 cm/¾ in) of fresh root ginger, peeled and crushed
3 cloves garlic, crushed
3 ripe, red tomatoes, skinned and finely chopped
1–2 sticks (about 4 cm/1½ in each) cinnamon
6 cardamom pods, cracked
15 ml (1 tbsp) ground turmeric
15 ml (1 tbsp) medium curry powder or fish masala (see note)
4 potatoes, peeled, parboiled and quartered
5 ml (1 tsp) garam masala (see right)
30 ml (2 tbsp) chopped fresh coriander leaves
salt

GARNISH
fresh coriander leaves

NOTE: This is usually available in ready-mixed form.

Cut the fish into chunks and set aside. Heat the butter and oil and cook the onions gently for about 5–10 minutes or until glossy. Stir in the fish, ginger and garlic. Stir in the tomatoes, cinnamon, cardamom, turmeric, curry powder, potatoes,

masala, potatoes and a sprinkling of salt. Cover and simmer for about 10–15 minutes, adding a little water if necessary, until the fish is just cooked through and the potatoes are tender. Stir in the garam masala and the chopped coriander leaves. Season to taste.

Garnish with coriander leaves and serve with fluffy white rice, mango chutney and lime pickle.
SERVES 4–6

GARAM MASALA

This is an Indian spice mix, used for flavouring during cooking, at the end of cooking time or for sprinkling over food at table. It is typically used in North Indian cooking, and the mix varies enormously from household to household.

1 stick (about 4 cm/1½ in) cinnamon, broken into pieces
45 ml (3 tbsp) cumin seeds
45 ml (3 tbsp) coriander seeds
15 ml (1 tbsp) black peppercorns
15 ml (1 tbsp) cardamom pods, cracked
2.5 ml (½ tsp) whole cloves
1.25 ml (¼ tsp) freshly grated nutmeg

Using a heavy pan and shaking all the time, toast the cinnamon pieces, cumin and coriander seeds, the peppercorns, cardamom and cloves for a few minutes until fragrant. Turn out and allow to cool. Add the nutmeg and grind together in a clean coffee mill or spice mill used exclusively for this purpose. Seal tightly to store. This spice mix will keep for months.

MALAYSIAN CHICKEN CURRY

The subtle spices used in this recipe permeate this dish. Prepare it the day before to ensure the most successful mingling of the exotic flavours.

750 g–1 kg (1¾–2¼ lb) chicken pieces
15–30 ml (1–2 tbsp) Malaysian chilli paste (see page 9)
60 ml (4 tbsp) ground coriander
30 ml (2 tbsp) ground cinnamon
125 g (4 oz) finely chopped onion
30 g (1 oz) fresh root ginger, peeled and crushed
4 fat cloves garlic, crushed
2 stalks lemon grass (see page 11)
60 ml (4 tbsp) oil
1 star anise
5 ml (1 tsp) cumin seeds
500 ml (17 fl oz) thin coconut milk (see page 11)
250 ml (8 fl oz) thick coconut milk (see page 11)
125 g (4 oz) tomato, skinned and chopped
salt

Trim and wash the chicken pieces and pat dry using paper towels. Pound together the chilli paste, coriander, cinnamon, onion, ginger, garlic and lemon grass to form a paste. Mix well with the chicken. Heat the oil in a heavy saucepan. Add the star anise, cumin seeds and chicken pieces, and fry for about 5 minutes. Add the thin coconut milk, bring to a simmer, then cook gently, covered, for approximately 40 minutes or until tender. Add the thick coconut milk, the chopped tomato and a little salt. Simmer until very tender. Season to taste.
SERVES 4–6

COCONUT CHICKEN CURRY

This curry, with its use of coconut milk, originates in Thailand. Using milk with the desiccated coconut produces a wonderfully rich result, and the meatiness of chicken thighs is excellent for a curry. It's a perfect dish for a sophisticated dinner party.

12 chicken thighs
15 ml (1 tbsp) mild curry powder (see page 71)
250 ml (8 fl oz) milk
100 g (3½ oz) desiccated coconut
1 clove garlic, crushed
a chunk (about 2 cm/¾ in) of fresh root ginger, peeled and crushed
30 ml (2 tbsp) sunflower oil
15 g (½ oz) butter
1 medium onion, very thinly sliced
15 ml (1 tbsp) flour
5 ml (1 tsp) ground cumin
5 ml (1 tsp) ground coriander
250 ml (8 fl oz) chicken stock
salt and pepper

GARNISH
4–6 spring onions, thinly sliced
fresh coriander leaves

Trim and wash the chicken thighs and pat dry using paper towels. Rub 5 ml (1 tsp) of the curry powder and a little salt and pepper into the chicken. Allow to stand while preparing the coconut milk.

Warm the milk, then mix with the coconut. Process or blend together. Turn into a strainer, then press out as much liquid as possible. Discard the coconut.

Stir the garlic and ginger into the coconut milk. In a large pan heat the oil. Then add the chicken and brown, in stages if necessary. Remove using a slotted spoon. Add the butter to the pan. When melted, add the onion and cook gently for 5–10 minutes or until softened. Stir in the flour, the remaining curry powder, the cumin and coriander.

Gradually stir in the hot stock and keep stirring until smooth and thickened. Return the chicken and any juices to the pan. Cover and cook gently for 30 minutes or until very tender. Remove the chicken pieces using a slotted spoon. Stir the coconut milk into the pan and, stirring all the time, bring to the boil. Check seasoning. Return the chicken pieces to the sauce and allow to heat through.

Sprinkle the sliced spring onion and the coriander leaves over the chicken to garnish. Serve with Basmati Rice Pilaf (see right) and Thai Cucumber Salad (see below).
SERVES 6

THAI CUCUMBER SALAD

30 ml (2 tbsp) sugar
5 ml (1 tsp) salt
100 ml (3½ fl oz) rice vinegar or white vinegar
30 ml (2 tbsp) thinly sliced, fresh red chillies
125 ml (½ cup) sliced spring onion
250 ml (1 cup) thinly sliced cucumber
fresh coriander leaves

Mix the sugar and salt with the vinegar until dissolved. Then add the chillies, onion and cucumber. Sprinkle with some coriander leaves and serve with Satay (see page 56).
SERVES 4–6

BASMATI RICE PILAF

200 g (7 oz) basmati rice
60 g (2 oz) butter
2 medium onions, finely chopped
3–4 fresh green chillies, seeds removed, finely chopped
1–2 cloves garlic, crushed
5 ml (1 tsp) salt
60 ml (4 tbsp) water
2.5 ml (½ tsp) garam masala (see page 65)

Soak the rice in plenty of water for 30 minutes. Bring a large saucepan of water to the boil. In a medium saucepan, heat half the butter, add the onion and cook gently, covered, for about 5 minutes or until it has softened. Stir in the chillies and garlic. Drain the rice, then gradually add to the saucepan of boiling water. Boil, uncovered, for 5 minutes, then drain and stir the rice into the onion mixture. Now add the salt and 60 ml (4 tbsp) water and dot with the remaining butter. Cover tightly and cook gently for about 10 minutes or until cooked through.

Finally, fluff up with a fork and stir in the garam masala.
SERVES 4–6

CHICKEN CURRY

In the tradition of the Cape Malay style of cooking, this curry goes well with a sweet chutney and a sharp pickle.

30 ml (2 tbsp) sunflower oil
2 medium onions, chopped
3 sticks (about 4 cm/1½ in each) cinnamon
3 cardamom pods, cracked
1 kg (2¼ lb) chicken pieces
2.5 ml (½ tsp) crushed garlic
2.5 ml (½ tsp) peeled, crushed root ginger
3 ripe, red tomatoes, skinned and chopped

30 ml (2 tbsp) mild curry powder
or chicken masala (see note)
6 curry leaves
250 ml (8 fl oz) water
4 potatoes, peeled and cubed
salt

GARNISH
fresh coriander leaves

NOTE: This is usually available in ready-mixed form from Indian grocers and supermarkets.

Heat the oil in a heavy saucepan and braise the onions slowly, together with the cinnamon and cardamom, for about 10 minutes.

Now add the chicken, garlic and ginger. Cover and cook for about 20 minutes or until a good colour. Add the tomatoes, masala and curry leaves and mix together well. Sprinkle with salt and pour in the water. Add the potatoes and cook gently for a further 25–30 minutes or until everything is tender.

Serve with steamed rice or Roti breads (see page 63), Dhal (see below), dried fruit chutney, mango pickle, a tomato and onion sambal and slices of freshly fried aubergine (see below right).
SERVES 4–6

COCONUT CHICKEN CURRY SERVED WITH BASMATI RICE PILAF AND THAI CUCUMBER SALAD (ALL PAGE 66)

DHAL

*This is an Indian recipe
which makes an excellent side dish
served with curry.*

250 g (9 oz) brown or red lentils
30 ml (2 tbsp) sunflower oil
5 ml (1 tsp) black mustard seeds
1 medium onion, thinly sliced
2 cloves garlic, crushed
a chunk (about 2 cm/¾ in) of fresh
root ginger, peeled and crushed
5 ml (1 tsp) garam masala
(see page 65)
5 ml (1 tsp) ground turmeric

2 fresh chillies, chopped
500 ml (17 fl oz) water
5 ml (1 tsp) salt

Soak the lentils for 30 minutes. Skim off any grit, rinse and drain. Set aside. Heat the oil in a suitable saucepan. Add the mustard seeds and fry for 1–2 minutes until they start to pop. Add the onion, garlic and ginger, and cook very gently until golden, but not browned. Stir in the garam masala and turmeric, and cook until fragrant. Add the lentils, chillies, water and salt. Bring to a simmer and cook to the consistency of a purée, until the lentils are very tender and the liquid has evaporated. If the mixture is too thick, dilute with boiling water. Season to taste and serve.
SERVES 6–8

FRIED AUBERGINES

2 medium aubergines
salt
oil for frying

Slice the aubergines thinly, salt lightly and place in a colander to drain for about an hour. Rinse, drain and dry the slices, using paper towels; then fry in medium to hot oil for about 5 minutes on each side, or until lightly browned and tender.
SERVES 4–6

SOSATIES

A South African favourite, this dish originates from the satays of the Malay slaves who were brought to the country by the Dutch during the seventeenth century.

45 ml (3 tbsp) curry powder
(see page 71)
250 ml (8 fl oz) white wine vinegar
6 bay leaves or 12 lemon leaves
250 ml (8 fl oz) dry red wine
10 ml (2 tsp) ground coriander
5 ml (1 tsp) ground ginger
5 ml (1 tsp) ground allspice
1.25 ml (¼ tsp) pepper
10 ml (2 tsp) salt
30 ml (2 tbsp) soft brown sugar
2 kg (4½ lb) leg of lamb,
boned and cubed
3 medium onions, sliced
100 g (3½ oz) dried apricots, halved
2 cloves garlic, chopped

Mix the curry powder with a small amount of the vinegar to form a paste. Gradually add the remaining vinegar. Turn into a saucepan, add the bay or lemon leaves and bring to the boil. Immediately remove from the heat and allow to cool. Add the wine and set the sauce aside. Mix together the spices, salt and sugar and rub into the meat. Place in a bowl together with the onions, apricots and garlic. Pour the curry sauce over the meat and allow to marinate in the refrigerator for one or two days, turning occasionally.

Thread the meat, onions and apricots onto wooden skewers. Cook under a preheated grill or over hot coals for about 10 minutes on each side until well browned and tender. Brush frequently with the marinade to keep the sosaties moist and flavourful.

Serve with the traditional Yellow Rice and Raisins (see below).
SERVES 8–10

YELLOW RICE & RAISINS

200 g (7 oz) long-grain rice
500 ml (17 fl oz) water
5 ml (1 tsp) butter
5 ml (1 tsp) salt
15 ml (1 tbsp) sugar
2.5 ml (½ tsp) turmeric
15 ml (1 tbsp) seedless raisins

Cover the rice with the water. Add the remaining ingredients and bring to the boil, stirring occasionally. Reduce the heat, cover and simmer for 20 minutes. Turn off the heat and allow to stand for another 5 minutes or until the liquid has been absorbed and the rice is tender. Serve with Sosaties (see left) or with Bobotie (see right).
SERVES 4–6

BOBOTIE

This is another traditional South African dish that shows the Dutch-Indonesian influence.

30 g (1 oz) butter
2 medium onions, sliced
1 kg (2¼ lb) lean, minced beef
300 ml (½ pint) milk
3 extra large eggs
2 slices bread, crusts removed, cubed
30 g (1 oz) chopped, dried apricots
1 apple, peeled and grated
30 g (1 oz) seedless raisins
30 g (1 oz) flaked almonds
30 ml (2 tbsp) apricot jam
15 ml (1 tbsp) curry powder
(see page 71)
30 ml (2 tbsp) lemon juice
10 ml (2 tsp) salt
1.25 ml (¼ tsp) pepper
6 fresh lemon leaves or bay leaves
1.25 ml (¼ tsp) turmeric

Melt the butter and cook the onion gently for 5–10 minutes or until pale golden. Add the meat and stir over a high heat until the meat changes colour. Remove from the heat. In a large bowl, beat together 60 ml (4 tbsp) of the milk and one egg. Add the bread, mashing together with a fork. Add the apricots, apple, raisins, almonds, jam, curry powder, lemon juice and salt and pepper and mix together well. Add the meat and mix lightly with a fork. Turn into an oiled, ovenproof dish and spread evenly. Roll the leaves and press into the meat mixture. Bake the bobotie, uncovered, at 180 °C (350 °F; gas 4) for about 30 minutes.

Beat the remaining eggs with the remaining milk and the turmeric and pour over the baked meat mixture. Now bake for a further 15 minutes or until set. Serve with steamed rice and chutney.
SERVES 6

BOBOTIE SERVED WITH YELLOW RICE AND RAISINS (BOTH PAGE 68)

FRUITY LAMB CURRY

This is a wonderfully substantial curry, just the sort of fare for cold winter nights.

1.5 kg (3½ lb) shoulder of lamb chops
oil for frying
2 medium onions, thinly sliced
500 ml (17 fl oz) water
a chunk (about 2 cm/¾ in) of fresh
root ginger, peeled and chopped
2 cloves garlic, chopped
5 ml (1 tsp) turmeric
45 ml (3 tbsp) curry powder
(see page 71)
15 ml (1 tbsp) sugar
125 ml (4 fl oz) brown or
white vinegar
1 fresh chilli, seeded and chopped
3 bay leaves
2 sticks (about 4 cm/1½ in each)
cinnamon
6 peppercorns
6 allspice
6 cardamom pods, cracked
3 ripe tomatoes, skinned
and chopped
3 bananas, sliced
90 g (3 oz) sultanas
1 large apple, grated
30 ml (2 tbsp) fruity chutney
salt and pepper

Trim any excess fat from the lamb. Place the lamb in a heavy saucepan and brown it in its own fat, adding oil if necessary. Remove using a slotted spoon and season with salt.

In the same saucepan, add the onions. Cook gently until golden brown, adding oil if necessary. Add 375 ml (13 fl oz) water and simmer for 20 minutes. Meanwhile, using a pestle and mortar, pound the ginger and garlic together with a little salt to form a paste. Mix this together with the turmeric, curry powder and sugar. Gradually stir in the vinegar and 125 ml (4 fl oz) water. Add the mixture to the meat together with the chilli, bay leaves, spices, tomatoes, bananas, sultanas, apple and fruity chutney. Simmer gently for about an hour or until very tender. Adjust seasoning if necessary. Serve with steamed rice and a choice of accompaniments: fruity chutney, mango pickle, chopped tomato and onion, sliced bananas mixed with thick yoghurt and crisply fried poppadoms.
SERVES 6

FRUITY PORK CURRY

This is an elegant curry, enriched with cream and sweetened with dried fruits. It makes a fine main course for a small dinner party.

15 ml (1 tbsp) sunflower oil
30 g (1 oz) unsalted butter
1 kg (2¼ lb) diced, lean pork
2 medium onions, finely chopped
1 clove garlic, crushed
2 large, ripe tomatoes
250 ml (8 fl oz) chicken stock
1 stick (about 4 cm/1½ in) cinnamon
5 ml (1 tsp) ground cumin
5 ml (1 tsp) ground coriander
10 ml (2 tsp) curry powder
(see page 71)
30 g (1 oz) soaked apricots, sliced
30 g (1 oz) soaked, dried figs, sliced
3 bananas, sliced
15 ml (1 tbsp) mango chutney
60 ml (4 tbsp) single (thin) cream
a squeeze of lemon juice
salt and freshly ground black pepper

GARNISH
fresh coriander leaves

Heat the oil and half the butter in a heavy saucepan and brown the meat in batches, adding a little more oil if necessary. Remove the browned meat from the pan. Add the remaining butter to the pan, add the onion and cook gently until softened. Stir in the garlic. Return the browned meat to the pan. Halve the tomatoes and grate each half directly into the pan, discarding the skin. Add the stock and the spices and bring to the boil, then reduce the heat, cover tightly and simmer very gently for 40 minutes or until very tender. Stir occasionally and, halfway through, add the fruit and chutney. Once the meat is tender, stir in the cream and lemon juice. Season to taste and garnish with coriander leaves. Serve with Coconut Rice (see page 61), mango chutney and a bowl of thick yoghurt, sprinkled with cinnamon.
SERVES 4–6

THAI GREEN CHICKEN CURRY

Thai curries are stir-fried, quickly cooked and use fresh herbs, in contrast to the long-simmered, spicier Indian curries. Often you can buy the green curry paste ready-made from supermarkets or specialist spice shops, which makes it a quick dish. If not, prepare it at home when you have the time.

1 small aubergine, about 100 g
(3½ oz), diced
30 ml (2 tbsp) sunflower oil
500 g (18 oz) skinned, filleted
chicken breast, sliced
30 ml (2 tbsp) green curry paste
(see right)
500 ml (17 fl oz) thick coconut milk
(see page 11)
4 fresh green chillies, thinly sliced
4 fresh kaffir lime leaves, finely
chopped or 15 ml (1 tbsp) finely
chopped lime or lemon rind
12 fresh basil leaves, coarsely
shredded
30 ml (2 tbsp) Thai fish sauce
(see page 11)
5 ml (1 tsp) sugar

GARNISH
fresh basil leaves and sliced chillies

First salt the diced aubergine, weigh down for an hour, then rinse and pat dry. Heat the oil in a heavy saucepan and stir-fry the sliced chicken, then remove it using a slotted spoon. Stir-fry the aubergine, adding a little more oil if necessary. Remove and set aside. Add the curry paste to the pan and fry gently. Pour in half the coconut milk and return the chicken and the aubergine to the pan. Gradually pour in the remaining coconut milk and, stirring constantly, add the remaining ingredients. Simmer gently for 5–10 minutes or until the chicken is just cooked. Garnish with basil and chillies.
SERVES 4

GREEN CURRY PASTE

9 fresh, green chillies, finely chopped
15 ml (1 tbsp) lemon grass
(see page 11)
1 small onion, finely chopped
15 ml (1 tbsp) finely chopped garlic
3 fresh coriander roots, chopped
(optional)
15 ml (1 tbsp) ground coriander
seeds
5 ml (1 tsp) ground cumin seeds
2.5 ml (½ tsp) ground white
peppercorns
5 ml (1 tsp) finely chopped lime or
lemon rind
10 ml (2 tsp) shrimp paste
(see page 11)
5 ml (1 tsp) salt

Use a mortar and pestle or pound the ingredients together in a small food processor to form a thick paste.

BEEF CURRY

Here's an easy-to-prepare basic curry made in the Indian manner. Choose the strength of curry powder to suit your palate – home-made (see page 71) or the best of the ready-made varieties available.

1 kg (2¼ lb) lean beef (boneless shin),
cut into cubes of 2 cm (¾ in)
45 ml (3 tbsp) flour
30 ml (2 tbsp) sunflower oil
30 g (1 oz) butter
2 medium onions, thinly sliced
1 clove garlic, crushed
1 litre (1¾ pints) beef stock
2 bay leaves
30 ml (2 tbsp) curry powder
(see page 71)
15 g (½ oz) seedless raisins
salt and freshly ground black pepper

steamed rice
poppadoms
sweet chutney
hot lemon or mango pickle

sliced banana or apple moistened
with lemon juice
chopped tomato and onion
moistened with vinegar

Wash the beef cubes and pat dry using paper towels. Toss the beef cubes in the flour. Heat the oil and butter in a suitable heavy saucepan, and brown the beef in batches. Remove using a slotted spoon and season to taste. Add the sliced onion to the pan and cook gently for about 5–10 minutes until softened and golden. If necessary, add a little of the stock to prevent the onion from catching. Stir in the garlic.

Return the meat to the saucepan and pour in the stock. Add the bay leaves, reduce the heat and cover. Simmer gently for about an hour. Stir in the curry powder and simmer for another hour or until the meat is very tender. Add the raisins and cook for a further 5 minutes or until plump. Season to taste and serve with rice and accompaniments.

SERVES 6

CURRY POWDER

*The ready-made blends
of curry powder which are available
vary as much as the different mixes
of garam masala. In Indian cooking
there are hundreds of different kinds
of curry powder, depending on the
region or the particular dish.
Here's one way of making it –
if you want it hotter,
use more chillies.*

60 ml (4 tbsp) coriander seeds
15 ml (1 tbsp) cumin seeds
3 dried red chillies, stems removed
5 ml (1 tsp) ground ginger
10 ml (2 tsp) ground turmeric
1.25 ml (¼ tsp) mustard seeds
1.25 ml (¼ tsp) fenugreek seeds
a stick (about 2 cm/¾ in) of cinnamon

FRUITY PORK CURRY (PAGE 70) SERVED WITH COCONUT RICE (PAGE 61)

3 cardamom pods
5 ml (1 tsp) black peppercorns
1 whole clove

Mix the various spices together and roast them at 180 °C (350 °F; gas 4) for approximately 10 minutes, or dry-roast in a frying pan, stirring often, until fragrant. Now grind the mixture in a clean coffee mill or in a special spice grinder.

Store the curry powder in an airtight container and preferably keep it in a cool dark place.

Vegetarian Dishes

Wholesome vegetarian dishes are an excellent addition to anyone's repertoire of menus. Spice boosts vegetables, giving them extra punch. This collection of recipes is really good, combining all sorts of vegetables with pulses and complex carbohydrates to come up with delicious results that are well balanced and healthy.

SUNDAY BRUNCH: *A Spicy Vegetable Omelette (page 77), herbal teas, preserves, wholewheat rolls and a tropical fruit bowl*

VEGETABLE CHILLI CASSEROLE

Spoon this delicious vegetable chilli onto hot brown rice or warm tortillas, and top with spoonfuls of thick, soured cream, chopped spring onion and grated cheese. Serve with a salad of shredded lettuce, chopped tomato and avocado dressed with oil and vinegar.

45 ml (3 tbsp) oil
1 medium onion, chopped
1 can (about 400 g/14 oz) tomatoes
300 g (11 oz) small, whole mushrooms
250 g (9 oz) cauliflower, broken into florets
250 g (9 oz) courgettes, thickly sliced
1 large green pepper, seeds removed, sliced
1 large red pepper, seeds removed, sliced
1 clove garlic, crushed
30 ml (2 tbsp) chilli powder (see page 9)
2 cans (about 400 g/14 oz each) pinto beans
salt and freshly ground black pepper

thick, soured cream
chopped spring onions
grated mild Cheddar cheese

Heat the oil in a heavy casserole and stir in the onion. Cook gently until softened. Drain the tomatoes and chop, setting aside the juice. Stir the tomatoes into the casserole and cook for 5–10 minutes. Add the mushrooms, cauliflower, courgettes, green and red pepper and garlic. Season lightly, then cover tightly and simmer for about 15 minutes or until the vegetables are tender-crisp. Mix the chilli powder with the reserved tomato juice and pour into the casserole. Add the beans and simmer for 10–15 minutes or until the vegetables are tender and the beans are piping hot. Season to taste and serve immediately.
SERVES 6

SPICED VEGETABLE STEW

This mix of vegetables, pulses and spices makes an excellent meal. Serve with steamed basmati rice and pass round a bowl of thick yoghurt.

45 ml (3 tbsp) sunflower oil
1 medium onion, chopped
1 medium carrot, chopped
1 stick celery, chopped
1 green pepper, chopped
2 cloves garlic, crushed
5 ml (1 tsp) ground cumin
5 ml (1 tsp) ground coriander
15 ml (1 tbsp) curry powder (see page 71)
1 large aubergine, cubed
250 g (9 oz) pumpkin, cubed
4 small courgettes, sliced thickly
150 g (5 oz) cauliflower florets
4 ripe, red tomatoes, skinned and chopped
125 g (4 oz) cooked green lentils
125 g (4 oz) cooked butter beans
2 sticks (about 4 cm/1½ in each) cinnamon
4 cardamom seeds
375 ml (13 fl oz) vegetable stock or water
200 g (7 oz) raw, well-washed red lentils
salt and freshly ground black pepper

GARNISH
fresh coriander leaves

Heat the oil in a heavy saucepan and soften the onion, carrot, celery and green pepper gently. Stir in the garlic. Mix the cumin, coriander and curry powder. Stir into the softened vegetables. Add the aubergine, pumpkin, courgettes, cauliflower, tomatoes, cooked lentils and beans. Add seasoning and the cinnamon and cardamom. Pour in the stock and stir in the raw red lentils. Cover and cook for 30 minutes or until the vegetables are tender.

Season to taste and garnish with fresh coriander leaves.
SERVES 6

CURRIED LENTILS WITH EGGS

This is the kind of easy dish that will come in handy when you haven't planned what to cook, as it makes use of typical store cupboard ingredients. Probably the only ingredient that does need a little thought is the fresh coriander.

500 g (18 oz) brown or green lentils
60 ml (4 tbsp) oil
1 medium onion, finely chopped
2 cloves garlic, crushed
15 ml (1 tbsp) curry powder (see page 71)
5 ml (1 tsp) ground cumin
5 ml (1 tsp) ground coriander
1 can (about 400 g/14 oz) tomatoes, crushed
6 extra large hard-boiled eggs, halved

GARNISH
fresh coriander leaves

Soak the lentils for approximately 30 minutes, skim off the grit and drain. Heat the oil and cook the onion and then the garlic until softened. Stir in the spices. Add the washed and drained lentils, the crushed tomatoes together with the juice and enough water to cover. Bring to a simmer, cover and cook gently for 45 minutes or until soft, adding more water if necessary.

Purée half roughly with a potato masher, then mix the lot together and season to taste. Turn into a bowl, add the hard-boiled eggs and garnish with coriander. Serve with steamed brown rice, thick yoghurt and chutney of your choice.
SERVES 6

SOYA BEAN CURRY

*Soya beans are considered the prince
of pulses, because of their high
protein content. The disadvantage
is that they are very bland tasting.
They cry out for spice to give them
character and this recipe does
that most successfully.*

30 g (1 oz) butter
60 ml (4 tbsp) oil
3 medium onions, thinly sliced
4 cloves garlic, crushed
a chunk (about 2 cm/¾ in) of fresh
root ginger, peeled and chopped
20 ml (4 tsp) ground coriander
20 ml (4 tsp) ground cumin
5 ml (1 tsp) ground cinnamon
2.5 ml (½ tsp) ground cloves
1.25 ml (¼ tsp) ground nutmeg
1 can (about 400 g/14 oz) tomatoes,
crushed
125 ml (4 fl oz) cooking liquid
(from the soya beans)
375 g (12 oz) cooked soya beans
5 ml (1 tsp) curry leaf masala or
medium curry powder (see page 71)
juice of half a lemon
salt and cayenne pepper

thick yoghurt, flavoured with crushed
garlic and chopped mint

GARNISH
crisply fried onions
chopped, unsalted peanuts or
cashews
chopped, fresh coriander leaves

Heat half the amount of butter and
oil and cook half the onions until
brown and crisp. Remove and set
aside for garnishing.

Heat the remaining oil and butter
and cook the remaining onion
gently until softened, but still pale
in colour. Stir in the garlic, ginger
and spices. Stir in the crushed
tomatoes together with the juice
from the can and the cooking
liquid. Add the cooked beans and
simmer for about 20 minutes. Stir
in the curry leaf masala and lemon
juice. Add salt and cayenne pepper
to taste and cook for a few more
minutes. Turn into a bowl or onto a
platter and garnish with the onions,
nuts and coriander leaves.

Serve with steamed wholewheat
rice and a sauce of thick yoghurt
mixed with crushed garlic and
some chopped mint.
SERVES 4–6

CURRIED SOYA BAKE

*Another recipe that gives the soya
bean the full flavour treatment,
resulting in a tasty, wholesome dish.*

450 g (1 lb) cooked soya beans
1 bunch leeks
2 sticks celery
45 ml (3 tbsp) oil
2 cloves garlic, crushed
15 ml (1 tbsp) curry leaf masala or
medium curry powder (see page 71)
60 g (2 oz) wholewheat breadcrumbs
2 carrots, grated
1 large sweet potato, grated
5 ml (1 tsp) ground coriander
30 ml (2 tbsp) chopped parsley
30 g (1 oz) wheat germ
2 extra large eggs, beaten
salt and freshly ground black pepper
sunflower seeds for sprinkling
oil for drizzling

Mash the cooked beans roughly and
set aside. Wash the leeks and celery,
and slice thinly. Heat the oil and
cook the vegetables gently until
softened, but not browned. Add the
garlic and masala. Mix together
with the mashed beans and the
remaining ingredients, seasoning
each ingredient as you add. Pack
into a well-oiled, fairly deep ovenproof dish (or loaf tin), smoothing
the top. Sprinkle generously with
sunflower seeds, pressing them into
the mixture. Drizzle with oil and
bake at 190 °C (375 °F; gas 5) for
an hour until browned and firm to
the touch. If using a loaf tin, leave
to stand for about 5 minutes. Then
loosen the edges with a knife and
turn out onto a warm serving dish.

Serve with Spiced Brown Rice
(see below), chutney and a herbed
tomato and onion salad.
SERVES 4

SPICED BROWN RICE

200 g (7 oz) brown rice
30 ml (2 tbsp) oil
1 medium onion, thinly sliced
1 clove garlic, chopped
1 litre (1¾ pints) water
3 cardamom seeds
1 whole clove
2 peppercorns
1–2 sticks (about 4 cm/1½ in each)
cinnamon
15 ml (1 tbsp) butter
5 ml (1 tsp) salt

Rinse the rice under cold water.
Heat the oil and sauté the onion
gently until softened and pale
golden. Add the rice and stir-fry for
a few minutes. Stir in the garlic. Add
the water, spices, butter and salt.
Bring to a simmer, then reduce the
heat, cover tightly and cook gently
for 30 minutes or until the rice is
tender and the liquid is absorbed.
SERVES 4

SPICED INDONESIAN VEGETABLES

*Oriental cooks certainly
have a way with vegetables,
and this Indonesian stir-fry, perked
up with chilli, makes a nice change
from the more usual Chinese version.
I've suggested using lemon rind,
but if you do have lemon grass
(see page 11), this would make
the dish more authentic.*

500 g (18 oz) mix of raw vegetables
(use shredded cabbage, sliced green
beans, carrots, cauliflower and
broccoli florets)
250 ml (8 fl oz) vegetable stock
15 ml (1 tbsp) rice vinegar or
white wine vinegar
5 ml (1 tsp) sugar
grated rind of a lemon

MARINADE
2–3 fresh chillies, crushed
1 clove garlic, crushed
a chunk (about 2 cm/¾ in) of fresh
root ginger, peeled and crushed
4–6 spring onions, chopped
5 ml (1 tsp) ground turmeric
2.5 ml (½ tsp) salt

Pound all the ingredients for the
marinade together to a fairly coarse
consistency using a pestle and
mortar. Coat the vegetables with the
marinade and leave to stand for
1–2 hours at room temperature.

Heat the stock in a wide saucepan or wok and add the vinegar,
sugar and lemon rind. Bring to a
simmer and stir in the prepared
vegetables. Keep stirring and cook
for a few minutes or until tender-
crisp. Remove to a bowl using a
slotted spoon and keep warm.

Reduce the remaining cooking
liquid over a high heat until it has
thickened slightly, before pouring it
over the vegetables.

Serve with fragrant steamed rice
and pass round Indonesian soy
sauce and chilli sauce.

SERVES 3–4

SPICED INDONESIAN VEGETABLES (THIS PAGE)

THAI STIR-FRIED VEGETABLES (PAGE 77); VEGETARIAN COUSCOUS (THIS PAGE)

VEGETARIAN COUSCOUS

Robust, earthy vegetables combined with couscous make a wonderfully comforting dish that should satisfy even a meat-lover.

VEGETABLES
60 ml (4 tbsp) olive oil
2 large onions, cut into half-moons
750 g (1¾ lb) pumpkin, peeled and diced
500 g (18 oz) carrots, peeled and diced
500–750 ml (17 fl oz–1¼ pints) vegetable stock or water
1 can (about 400 g/14 oz) chickpeas, drained
90 g (3 oz) seedless raisins, blanched
a chunk (about 2 cm/¾ in) of fresh root ginger, peeled and crushed
10 ml (2 tsp) clear honey
5 ml (1 tsp) ground cinnamon
2.5 ml (½ tsp) ground allspice
5 ml (1 tsp) chilli powder
salt

COUSCOUS
1.25 litres (2¼ pints) vegetable stock
a pinch of saffron
45 ml (3 tbsp) olive oil
15 ml (1 tbsp) ground cinnamon
2.5 ml (½ tsp) ground nutmeg
500 g (18 oz) couscous
(available from most supermarkets)

To cook vegetables, heat oil in a heavy saucepan. Add onions and cook gently for 10 minutes or until softened, but not browned. Add pumpkin and carrots, and cook for 15 minutes, stirring often, until starting to soften. Add the remaining ingredients and simmer for about 10–15 minutes or until vegetables are tender. Season to taste. To make couscous, add saffron to stock and bring to the boil, then reduce heat and simmer for a few minutes. Add oil, cinnamon and nutmeg. Place couscous in a bowl and pour over hot stock. Cover and leave for 5 minutes, then fluff with a fork.
SERVES 6–8

BAKED SPICED VEGETABLES & BROWN RICE

This layered casserole of vegetables and brown rice makes a satisfying, good-tasting meal.

375 g (12 oz) freshly cooked brown rice

SPICED VEGETABLES
45 ml (3 tbsp) sunflower oil
1 medium onion, chopped
1 medium carrot, chopped
3 cardamom seeds
1 stick (about 4 cm/1½ in) cinnamon
2 cloves garlic, crushed
5 ml (1 tsp) ground cumin
5 ml (1 tsp) ground coriander
15 ml (1 tbsp) curry powder (see page 71)
500 g (18 oz) ripe, red tomatoes, skinned and chopped
500 g (18 oz) peeled pumpkin, chopped

375 ml (13 fl oz) vegetable stock
or water
200 g (7 oz) raw, well-washed
red lentils
salt and freshly ground black pepper

GARNISH
fresh coriander leaves

Heat the oil in a heavy saucepan and soften the onion and carrot gently. Stir in the cardamom seeds, the cinnamon and garlic and cook for 1–2 minutes. Then stir in the cumin, coriander and curry powder. Add the tomatoes and cook gently for about 5 minutes. Add the pumpkin, stock, lentils and seasoning. Cover and cook for 30 minutes or until the vegetables are tender. Season to taste and strew with coriander leaves.

Layer with the cooked brown rice in an oiled baking dish. Cover with oiled, greaseproof paper and bake at 180 °C (350 °F; gas 4) for 20 minutes or until piping hot.

Garnish with coriander leaves and serve with hard-boiled eggs, dried fruit atjar, which is available from most supermarkets, and a bowl of thick yoghurt.
SERVES 4–6

SPICED VEGETABLE OMELETTE

This is a wonderful omelette, large enough to share with four or more if it's part of a meal. The spicing is Indian in origin.

VEGETABLES
60 ml (4 tbsp) sunflower oil
1 medium onion, chopped
1 clove garlic, crushed
1 large potato, diced
1 medium aubergine, diced
½ small cauliflower, broken
into florets
125 g (4 oz) green beans, thinly sliced
1 green pepper, chopped

1 large, ripe tomato, skinned
and chopped
5 ml (1 tsp) ground cumin
5 ml (1 tsp) ground coriander
2.5 ml (½ tsp) ground turmeric
1.25 ml (¼ tsp) chilli paste
(see pages 8–9)
250 ml (8 fl oz) water

EGGS
6 extra large eggs
30 ml (2 tbsp) water
5 ml (1 tsp) curry powder
(see page 71)
30 ml (2 tbsp) chopped, fresh
coriander leaves
30 g (1 oz) butter
100 g (3½ oz) feta cheese, diced
salt and freshly ground black pepper

GARNISH
fresh coriander leaves

Heat the oil in a heavy, wide pan, with a lid and ovenproof handles. First soften the onion, then stir in the garlic, then add the remaining vegetables. Mix the spices with the water and pour over the vegetables. Sprinkle over some seasoning, then cover and simmer until vegetables are tender. Uncover and cook over a high heat to evaporate any liquid.

Meanwhile, lightly whisk the eggs with the water, the curry, coriander and seasoning. Add the butter to the pan and when hot, pour in the eggs. Cook until the bottom has set and browned. Sprinkle with the feta cheese and slide under a hot grill until the top of the eggs has set and the cheese has softened nicely. Garnish with fresh coriander leaves and serve either hot or at room temperature.
SERVES 4–6

THAI STIR-FRIED VEGETABLES

Another oriental stir-fry that is excellent. Serve over steamed Thai rice, or try Chinese noodles for a change.

1 head broccoli
½ small cauliflower
125 g (4 oz) baby sweetcorn,
split lengthwise
5 ml (1 tsp) cornflour
30 ml (2 tbsp) Thai fish sauce
(see page 11)
15 ml (1 tbsp) lemon or lime juice
5 ml (1 tsp) sugar
a grinding of pepper
30 ml (2 tbsp) sunflower oil
1 small onion, thinly sliced
into half-moons
3 cloves garlic, finely chopped
90 g (3 oz) fresh bean sprouts
1 fresh red chilli, seeds removed,
chopped

Slice the stalks from the broccoli and cut into short, slim strips. Divide the heads of broccoli and cauliflower into tiny florets. Blanch the florets and corn by dropping them into a saucepan of boiling water. Allow the water to return to the boil, remove the florets and corn and drain well.

Slake the cornflour with the fish sauce, lemon or lime juice, the sugar and a grinding of pepper.

Heat the oil in a wok or other suitable pan. Add the thin slices of onion and stir-fry until pale golden and softened. Now add the garlic and stir-fry for 30 seconds. Increase the heat and add the broccoli, cauliflower and corn. Stir-fry for a few minutes until barely tender and still crisp. Stir in the bean sprouts, then the cornflour mixture. Mix well and finally add the chilli. Reduce the heat and continue to cook, stirring, for a few minutes more until heated through. Serve immediately over rice or noodles.
SERVES 6

Menus

This book offers recipes for many delectable dishes which will suit a variety of individual palates and moods. Try some of these menu suggestions to help you plan a selection of delightful occasions. Stars indicate recipes which have been included in the book.

SUNDAY BRUNCH

FOR SIX

Surprise your friends with a spicy brunch on a lazy Sunday. Go to the trouble of squeezing the juice, and provide lots of the best coffee. A platter of mixed tropical fruits – pawpaw, pineapple, kiwi and passion fruit, for instance – looks spectacular and tastes wonderful with a topping of thick yoghurt sprinkled with cinnamon.

Fresh orange juice
Tropical fruit bowl
Thick plain yoghurt with
cinnamon
Spiced Vegetable Omelette *
Wholewheat rolls, unsalted
butter and preserves
Herbal teas

SATURDAY LUNCH

FOR SIX

A robust soup and a hearty salad make a fitting lunch for a group of friends relaxing together on a lazy Saturday.

Spiced Lentil Soup *
Spicy Sausage and Chicken Liver
Pâté Salad *
Fresh fruit

AL FRESCO EATING

FOR EIGHT

A bountiful table of dishes at room temperature makes a beautiful spread for eating outdoors on a fine day.

Roasted Vegetable Salad with
Chilli Dressing *
Pitta breads
Shredded Chicken with Spiced
Walnut Sauce *
Brown Rice and Black Bean Salad
with Spicy Dressing*
A choice of sorbets and
sweet biscuits
Iced mint tea

A MEXICAN BARBECUE

FOR SIX TO EIGHT

Barbecue a fresh fish and serve it Mexican style for a hearty, healthy meal that's deliciously different.

Nachos with Salsa and
Guacamole *
Refried Beans *
Mexican-Style Barbecued Fish *
Warm tortillas
Spanish Rice *
Chilled watermelon wedges

A PASTA SUPPER

FOR FOUR

Mixed green salad with Italian
salami
Smoked Chicken and Chilli
Tagliatelle *
Sliced pears with shavings of
Parmesan
Espresso with amaretti biscuits

DINNER FOR SIX

This menu makes for a hearty yet elegant dinner. Set your best and brightest table and light lots of candles in a rainbow of colours.

Fresh Corn Terrine with Tomato
Chilli Sauce *
Stir-Fried Lamb and Chilli *
Spinach Rice *
Green salad
Fresh berries with fromage frais
and honey

WINTER SUNDAY SUPPER

FOR SIX

A hot, spicy, meal-in-one soup is just the thing for supper on a cold winter's night. Ladle into big bowls, then follow with a light salad and fresh fruit.

Moroccan-Style Fish Soup with
Couscous *
Harissa Paste *
Mixed green salad
Sliced oranges with cinnamon

A MALAYSIAN MEAL

FOR SIX

An exotic menu for a dinner party that will certainly delight your guests. Once again fresh fruit is the correct way to end a spicy meal.

Malaysian Chicken Curry *
Beef Rendang *
Sliced fresh cucumber
Halved hard-boiled eggs
Chilli sambal
Coconut Rice *
Chilled pineapple slices

A THAI DINNER

FOR SIX

Set aside the time to prepare this meal for friends who love good food.

Thai Cucumber Salad *
Thai-Style Beef Salad *
Pumpkin and Prawn Soup *
Thai Green Chicken Curry *
Steamed Thai rice
Thai Stir-Fried Vegetables *
Chilled cut fruits

AN ORIENTAL SUPPER

FOR FOUR

An easy-to-prepare stir-fry is the main course of this delicious meal.

Spicy Oriental Fish Soup *
Mango and Beef Stir-Fry *
Steamed rice
Spiced Indonesian Vegetables *
Chilled orange quarters
Green tea

CURRYING FRIENDS

FOR SIX

An aromatic curry with appropriate accompaniments is one of the best ways of feeding friends.

Crisp poppadums
Chicken Curry *
Dhal *
Steamed basmati rice
Sweet chutney
Hot pickle
Tomato and onion sambal
Fried Aubergine Slices *
Thick plain yoghurt with sliced
banana and cinnamon
Lemon tea

A MOROCCAN FEAST

FOR EIGHT

A steaming platter of couscous topped with a mix of meats and vegetables makes a marvellous main course for a dinner party.

Moroccan Couscous *
Harissa Paste *
Chilled orange slices with
chopped dates, cinnamon and
rose water

THE IBERIAN WAY

FOR SIX

A mix of robust Spanish and Portuguese dishes combines perfectly for a casual dinner party.

Spanish Shrimps in Spicy Tomato
Sauce *
Spicy Chicken Livers *
Crusty rolls
Portuguese-Style Mussel Pasta *
OR
Portuguese Piri-Piri Chicken *
Spanish Rice *
A mixed green salad
dressed with olive oil and red
wine vinegar
Crème caramel

A TEX-MEX PARTY

FOR SIXTEEN

Mexican beer
Spicy nachos and warm tortillas
Chilli and Beans for a Crowd *
Thick soured cream
Grated cheese
Tomato and Corn Salsa *
Lettuce and avocado salad
Chilled fresh fruits

A SEAFOOD BUFFET
FOR A CELEBRATION

FOR TEN TO TWELVE

Fresh oysters are ideal for a celebration. Ask your fishmonger to open them on the day. Allow four per person and serve with lemon and Tabasco. Make three times the amounts given in the spicy mussel and risotto recipe.

Chilled oysters on the half-shell
with lemon and Tabasco
Spicy Ceviche *
Baked Whole Fish with
Bouillabaisse Sauce *
Rouille *
Spicy Mussels *
Risotto *
Mixed green salad
Italian cheeses with fresh fruit
and crackers
Coffee and chocolates

COCKTAILS
FOR A CROWD

Cocktails are fun and guarantee the success of a party. Mix up jugs of margaritas and daiquiris and put out a bright spread of spicy cocktails. Allow two to three cocktails per person, and four to five portions of snacks. If you think that friends may stay late, prepare a large pot of the Chilli Corn Soup, and lots of strong coffee.*

Baby Corn with Chilli Dip*
Mussels on the Half-Shell with
Curry Mayonnaise *
Prawns with Chilli Seafood Sauce*
Taco Chips with Avocado Relish
and Tomato and Basil Salsa*
Grilled nachos
Spicy Cocktail Chicken Wings *
Barbecue Spareribs with Chinese
Chilli Sauce *